LeaderSINKSship

"A collection of real-life stories about how poor leadership sinks the life of organizations and their people"

Td
HOME OF VENTURES

Vishal Kulshrestha

Siddharth Gaur

HOME OF VENTURES

Publishing-in-support-of,

True Dreamster

www.truedreamster.com

Printed in India

#May2021

Dedicated to *Product* and *By Product*
of Accidental Leadership

Contents

INSPIRED BY TRUE EVENTS

The success of any organization or any team solely depends on its leaders, their behaviors, decisions, and choices they make. There are many books and literature available in the market which preaches what an ideal leader should do? But for a leader, it is more important than what a leader should not do.

According to Herzberg's Hygiene Factors at workplace opposite of 'Satisfaction' is not 'No Satisfaction', as there are factors like safety, cleanliness, office infrastructure, food that doesn't motivate the employee but its poor quality definitely demotivates them. Similarly, great practices followed by leaders may not inspire everyone but their wrong decisions, practices, policies, and behaviors impact everyone including the organization.

We have compiled this book with many stories after talking to people whose life or career was impacted by poor leadership or they made their careers worse by accidentally jumping into the leadership role. In any of the cases, poor leadership ruins the career of people with the inability to lead, take the right action, and decisions.

You might be thinking why it makes leaders so important when we have good processes in place, ISO/CMMI certifications, a well-experienced team, great infrastructure, etc. On one side, the organization of today does not have the luxury of stability since it faces an ever-increasing change in markets, customers, and technology. It needs to accept, adopt, and implement changes in the business model according to changing trends, technologies, customer preferences, and future needs. Further, the core business of the organization is constantly under threat today from the newcomers to the marketplace who are having a different business paradigm.

Another side is the current workforce which has the majority of millennial, highly energetic, multiskilled, and self-confident people. They don't work to survive, they work to thrive. They have high expectations from themselves and they seek challenges, yet work-life balance is of utmost importance to them.

That's where leadership comes, by stressing upon building an environment in which every employee develops and excels resulting in client growth which ultimately is organizational growth. However, based on our observation that somehow leaders are not able to influence and drive the team for high performance which is the focal point for achieving goals & success. In most of the organizations, leaders are doing all activities, operations, execution, day to day management other than leadership task by constantly conveying the purpose of the organization (known as vision), setting specific measurable objective (known as mission) to fulfill organization's purpose, and finally giving the strategic direction to the organization. And the majority of leadership issues are with mid-size organizations.

This pandemic has allowed us to connect with many people and compile their real-life experiences. Many of them have worked closely with C-level executives, founders, owners, department heads, line managers and many are working on these leadership roles. They shared great stories and experiences of success and failure of startups, mid-size or large organizations, projects, initiatives, and building teams, and every time the root cause was the leadership, either for success or failure.

When we started writing down on leadership, we talked with a lot of people, we realized the important question is not how to become a great leader or what a leader ideally should do? The burning question is why leaders fail, and interestingly failure of leadership is like sex, everyone knows about it, but nobody talks about it, everyone thinks they are the best leader and this is the problem with others. In other words, leadership failure is like diabetes, and hypertension, a lifestyle disease that cannot be just fixed but can be constantly managed and improved. So we decided to bring this naked truth, thanks for reading so far and we are sure that upcoming chapters you may find interesting and helpful.

Last, but not least the disclaimer, all characters of this book may appear real to you, yet, such resemblance you may find in every next workplace.

Vishal Kulshrestha & Siddharth Gaur

PROLOGUE

Hi, I am Nikhil, I am you, or I may be your reporting manager or your reporting manager's reporting manager or maybe your CEO. I can be anyone who is in a leadership position accidentally or by choice.

It's a story of my journey from a fresher to an entrepreneur where I learned the most useful and wonderful lessons of leadership. These lessons became the paving stones of my career as they didn't tell me what to do but on the contrary taught me what not to do, which nobody talks and tells.

Some of you may think this is only for the people who are in the leadership profile, "what's in it for me"? Then, you are living in a misconception. You may not be playing the role of designated leader but everyone is a leader of their life, leadership is not just limited to the title or designation or limited to the workplace. It's a way of life that how you want to deal with challenges in your life.

And no one competes to lose, we compete to win and you can only win when you are fighting from the front. People who are fighting from the front are leaders and you are one of them. Some people may not want to take the responsibility which comes with the title but it's a fact everyone has a desire to lead and people are constantly trying to find a way to lead whether in office, home, society, friends, or playground wherever it is feasible.

Sometimes the most obvious things are the least talked about and we mostly talk of the idealistic things, not about what can be done but what ought to be done. There is always a talk about what is a "right way" or "right thing" to do but seldom do we talk about what is not to be done. I believe that it is equally or more important to save yourself from certain pitfalls to become a good leader.

What are those most common pitfalls, what are the most common mistakes a leader tends to commit? I have learned them by my experiences as a leader and by observing the leaders I have worked with, which happened to be so fatal to an organization that led to the sinking of the whole ship.

I have tried to narrate every experience and incident as I have observed or gone through to the nearest to reality. I hope that you may be able to relate with them somewhere.

Every experience left me with many questions which I asked myself, I have shared them as well. Ask them to yourself. Hopefully, we together will be able to find all the answers.

Finally just remember I am Nikhil, a person around you......with one name or another you have come across. Today you might not be playing a designated role of a leader but one day you would be captain of your leader-ship journey, and it is important to learn how you can prevent your ship before it gets sink due to known or unknown mistakes.

1

Kaheen Kee Eent Kaheen Ka Roda, Bhaanumatee Ne Kunaba Joda

LEADERSHIP CHALLENGES IN TEAM BUILDING

"When a leader attempt to build a team by collecting or choosing people in a haywire manner"

It was very late. The wristwatch of Nikhil was showing 2 AM as he was in the lift reaching his house on the 32nd floor. His flight from New York landed an hour ago and as there was very less traffic at this hour, he was able to get home so early.

The door of the lift opened and he walked outside, there was complete silence, one of the most beautiful gifts of the night. He walked slowly towards his house with luggage in his hands and happiness of coming to roost in the heart.

The nameplate carved with silver letters read Mr. and Mrs. Chaudhary on the front door. His hand was about to press the doorbell when a thought struck his mind. He should not disturb Avantika and the kids.

He always had a spare key with him and it seems the right time to use it. He entered the house as slowly as possible, it felt like a thief sneaking in, thought came into his mind and a smile ran on his face.

He first went to the kid's room to see them. He had missed them very much. His daughters Ami and Jiya were smart girls of 12 and 20 years respectively. Their smartness is inherited from their mother Nikhil always thought. It was a delight for Nikhil to watch them sleep. He didn't go close to kiss them but turned around leaving the luggage in the hall to Avantika.

He slowly opened the door and went inside. Saw his wife Avantika asleep. Nikhil always loved to see people while they are sleeping, he wondered that is it with him or everybody else as well. Anyhow he never discussed it with anyone, not even with Avantika.

Despite getting rid of his three-piece suit he chose to sit on the armchair instead. Ahhh! It felt good. Good to be at home. Good to be in the armchair. Good to see Avantika sleeping.

He closed his eyes and dwelled on the memory lane. Today when he sees around he can consider himself as a successful man. A speaker and a coach of international repute. All luxuries in every walk of life. Two charming daughters and a loving and caring wife like Avantika. At the age of 51, he has all the things he had dreamt. Moreover the freedom to pursue his passion, to help leaders in making their ventures a success.

But this was not as easy as always. He was born in a lower-middle-class family in the small town of Uttar Pradesh.

His father was a shopkeeper who worked hard to keep them afloat. Mother was a spiritual lady with values and a kind heart. An elder sister who always inspired him to work hard.

Childhood was not easy. Everything came very hard be it new clothes, toys or even education. But harmony was always there in the family. They struggled for everything and fought together. But the only thing that came cheap was dreams. He dreamt of a future, a golden future. He got this encouragement from his sister, the will to fight for it from the father, and the belief of making it true from the mother.

He was good in the studies but it was his sister, Radhika who made him excel in that. He stood first in the district in the board exams and that time only decided to go to the IIT. Getting coaching was out of the question so he compensated that with hard work.

And then the day came when he got selected for the IIT. He still remembers the day. The family celebrated it as it was Deepawali. Mother offered pooja but the thing he never forgets was that when he saw his father crying in a corner alone for the very first time in life. The tears of joy and relief or like the battle has come to an end with a victory. Radhika was so proud and attended the greetings of neighbors and shared his success story with pride and a bit of exaggeration.

But then the even tougher battle started. Life at IIT was never easy from day one until Avantika came into his life. She was from a big city with a rather more profound background with her father being a Banker. How they met is a story of some other time but it could never have happened if Avantika hadn't initiated the talk with him as Nikhil wouldn't have dared to talk to a girl like Avantika. But since then she has been the backbone of his life. He wondered, that without her, he would not be able to achieve anything or pursue his passion.

He opened his eyes and saw Avantika. Still sleeping. A smile ran on his face as he remembered the day of their campus recruitment when he was about to have an interview the next day. He was nervous as anything but Avantika made him at ease. At least she thought that way, as he was not able to sleep the whole night and was watching Avantika sleeping the same way as today. She hasn't changed a bit.

How long he has come since that day. Seems like it started yesterday. The very first interview of his life for the very first job of his life.

He closed his eyes again and everything came as it is happening now.

It was a regular day but everything seems different. It was a day when he had to appear for the very first interview of his life. By the time Avantika woke up, he was done with his shave and shower and was getting dressed. Trying to fix the knot of the tie or the only tie which was a gift from Avantika. A sky blue tie with the yellow cross strips. A thought came to his mind that for two major events of your life you need to get dressed specifically and for both, you are nervous one is an interview and the other one is marriage.

But having a tie is one thing and knowing how to tie it is another. While he was struggling with it, Avantika helped him. She noticed the nervousness in him and tried to ease him out.

"Everything will be ok, you are thinking too much. You deserve it, you are among the brightest students of this college. People like me need to worry." said Avantika with a smile.

Her smile took all his worries away, how come she is always so calm thought Nikhil.

"Good luck Nikhil."

Now is the time to appear before the selection board of the most reputed IT Company in the Country. He entered the room. Greeted everyone with a gentle smile, sat in front of them which appeared to be a comfortable and formal posture. All that he has read about the best practices of appearance in an interview. There were three members in the selection board who appeared to be in their late fifties. And it started....

Tell me about yourself? One of the interviewers asked.

Haven't they read my resume at all? Anyway, what choice I had to answer.

I told them about my family and academic background but I doubt any of them was listening. So why ask? Or is it a ritual of every interview that needs to be performed like "Bhoomi Poojan" (Land Worship, The Bhumi Pujan is a customary ritual that is performed before initiating building construction) before constructing a house?

And then there were some technical questions which were not what I had studied but what they did in their company. I believed they knew about it, but they asked me anyway because that's what all they knew. It felt so because these questions were about outdated technologies that they must be working with.

Again why did they ask? Does it make them happy by believing that they still know more than the graduates of IIT of today? That they are still the gurus. The interview was intended to make them happy or to make the right selection for the right job, I wondered.

Suddenly one gentleman asked, "Why you want to join our company?" What?? Am I listening to it right? I wanted to answer, Sir, first of all, you didn't tell me anything about your company, what all I know is what Google Baba has told me. Secondly, I am not selecting companies I am looking for a job. It's you who have come to select employees.

Buttttt...Instead, I replied to what Avantika had instructed me and had rehearsed with me, as she knew that whether they ask anything or not, they would ask this for sure. It felt like your questionnaire was leaked sir, I giggled within. Next came, "Out of us three, who would you rather work with"?

Honestly none sir, not because I started hating you but I hardly know you to make this decision. Don't you know that? Or you just want to play poker with me? Does it matter with whom I work or you are concerned about what I will do? Am I in a position to choose my manager? Does your company give you a chance to choose the manager before joining?

Butttt...... Avantika was speaking from inside instead of me and all three of them seemed very impressed with my answer. Then again came some other brilliant questions.

Why do you want to do a job?

Are you ready to relocate?

Are you willing to travel abroad? And Avantika inside me kept replying.

The interview ended with big smiles and firm handshakes. And to my surprise by the evening I had the offer. The dream has come true. The path is set. Good job in a big company, big city, what else a small towner can dream of, but don't know why I was not happy at all. A thought came to my mind to call my parents, everyone will jump with joy especially Radhika but couldn't. It didn't feel like it. Something was missing. I wasn't happy at all.

After wandering here and there I went to my room late in the evening. From her face, I could tell, she had been waiting for me for a long time and was not happy about it.

"Where have you been?"

I was...

"What happened to your interview?"

It was...

"Were you selected? Yes or no"

"Yes."

"So for what you have been waiting for?"

Before I could say something she hugged me. She was happy. She was happy for me. Yes, she loved me.

"Let's plan a party"

"Avantika, I want to tell you something."

"What Nikhil, You don't seem happy at all. What happened?"

"I have decided not to accept the offer." Nothing came out of her mouth at once. She took some time to absorb what I had just said.

"Sit down. Let's talk Nikhil, looks like you are exhausted with the interview process."

It is even more alarming than Modiji's *"Mitron"* when your lady asks to talk.

"Tell me about it Nikhil, what happened?"

"It doesn't seem right to me, Avantika. It is not what I have dreamt for. They have offered me a job but not the opportunity. At least it didn't feel like when they described it."

"I wanted a chance Avantika, not a job. A chance to contribute, a chance of fair play. I wanted to be a part of a team where I have a role to play to win, not a spare part of big machinery. Since day one in this college, I want to implement what I am learning. I want to join a company which is a breathing entity, not a machine, who is looking for talent, not a mechanical tool."

"Not for once, it felt like they were looking for talent instead they were looking to fill some numbers. I didn't felt like they are looking for a contributor but instead, it was like they have come for a CSR activity by granting some jobs in their esteemed organization. All they wanted to hear was how badly I want to join them. It will be the biggest honour to serve them. I will remain obliged forever for this chance. I will work day and night without asking questions to prove their selection right."

"Then how come you get selected, Nikhil?"

"Avantika, it was you who got selected. It was you who was answering them. It was your mock interviews that made me through. I don't want it. I might be working but it's not what I wanted. It's not my dream. I am sorry Avantika I hope you will understand." I looked at her, her eyes seemed big, very big. It was anger or surprise I don't know.

Avantika didn't reply just said "Hmmmm."

"Hmmmm just Hmmmmm. Say something Avantika. If not then yell but I want something more than hmmm." She seems to be thinking. Thinking hard. It felt like years before she spoke.

"Now what will you do Nikhil." Finally, she responded.

"I don't know."

"Hadd hai, ye bhi main hi sochu Nikhil (You are expecting too much from me Nikhil, is this also I need to decide). You know you are such a moron. Let's eat something first, I haven't eaten the whole day." We were walking down the street together silently. I felt like a child who just got the result and was walking with his mother. She was looking at the horizon where the earth meets the sky.

I did not know when I fell asleep while thinking of my first encounter with the corporate world, 'my campus hiring days'. Everything started revolving like a movie in my eyes. That was the first stepping stone of my life, wherever I have reached today. In this materialistic world, it is considered "successful". It was my first learning experience of professional life, and initial experience always works as the foundation of your thoughts and learning.

I wanted to sleep till late in the morning, as tomorrow is Saturday and not only me, I believed other family members are also planning to take rest. Weekdays are hectic for everyone, be it kids or Avantika, all are having their own back-to-back schedule. My schedule was also very hectic during these three-day trips. From a business aspect, it was a very crucial trip for me, I was in Los Angeles to make the pitch for the third round of funding for my consulting startup.

Back-to-back meetings, endless (and some meaningless) questions of investors and their advisors, pinpointing on each corner of business whether it was impacting the business or not but they had to ask. Sometimes I feel it's a ritual if they don't ask won't look like-minded people or may lose their upper hand in business.

Although at the end of the day they are more interested in numbers, profit side of the Balance Sheet. By the grace of God and with the unprecedented efforts of all team members every year we are rocking in numbers. Those numbers impressed and increased the trust of investors, and I got the go-ahead for further expansion. This made my belief stronger that **"Numbers are closer to reality".**

A lot of things are getting piled up in my mind, and not allowing me to take long sleep and enjoy the weekend. Taking long sleep is a luxury for me during the weekend to have. Avantika and kids are in deep sleep, I am having a headache, maybe due to the tiring schedule or my mind is full of memories and an ongoing schedule. It looks like in the 50s our mind can process only one thing at a time.

I made a hot coffee and took some Raagi cookies (the Indian Brand), it's my morning mandatory ritual and without it, my day cannot be started. Taking a sip of coffee while sitting in my living room balcony is the most wonderful thing. Blue sky, beautiful view of golden gate bridge, seashore from my apartment in Seacliff.

While enjoying the coffee, I went into the past again, that how all my friends are very upset and on what basis I am refusing the offer from one multinational company. By that time news also reached my home town and my parents were also confused about how they can make me understand? For them it's not just about the job, it's more about pride in the society that their son got selected in such a big company from campus.

A middle-class mindset cannot think beyond the job, which is also not wrong, but the problem is we always focus on paycheck and perks. But hardly focus on growth and learning. Because that will build your career, a paycheck is always the outcome. And why to just blame the parents, Avantika's reaction was also similar, how can I leave such a lucrative opportunity? Frankly speaking, I was also thinking the same thing, when everyone is saying this is right for you. But why I am not willing to accept it? What is missing in this opportunity? On one side, my mind is saying that go and grab this and on another side, my heart is not agreeing with it.

However, today I know all the answers to all those unsolved puzzles and queries. Now I know why I haven't accepted that offer when everyone was saying "this is the right choice baby... aha". In totality the reason was very simple, "I was not influenced by the people who took my interview". Ya, that's it.

But it has a deeper meaning, in our days when we are about to pass the college, our practical knowledge is very limited and it is shared by our friends, classmates, professors, girlfriend/boyfriend and up to some extent parents. We listen and read stories about the big companies and brands and thrive to join those organizations by any means.

But when our first interaction happens with the representative of these companies during the interview, our imagination about that company gets actual shape. And it purely depends on the interviewer, how they leave the impression on our mind. During that time for people like us, they are the leader of the organization. Their knowledge and behaviour attract us.

Most of the time when we say that we didn't like the company, and if we go on root cause we didn't like the person who took our interview. Irrespective of the size of the organization, for me people who are selecting the candidates are the leader of the organization.

They represent the company, they are the people who become the role model, and candidates decide to join the organization or not. Hiring the right people is the most important part of building a strong team for leaders. The leader should act like a magnet, who can easily attract the candidate.

Selecting the wrong candidate is worse than finding none at all for any leader. According to the U.S. Department of Labor, the cost of a bad hiring decision can be as much as 30 percent of an employee's annual salary. Some of the most common mistakes by leaders while conducting the interview.

Bla-Bla-Bla

Most of the leaders don't take the interview, they are more interested in giving the interview. They just don't allow the candidate to speak, they keep talking and talking and want us to listen to what they have already framed in mind. Talking excessively squanders your opportunity to hear from the candidate. And asking predictable, softball questions like, "Tell me about yourself," or "Where do you see yourself in five years?" may reveal some of your candidates' interviewing skills, but you won't learn whether they have the actual skills and talent necessary to join your team.

Candidate Wahi jo mere man ko Bhaye (I like a candidate that pleases me)

It is hard to find "it" when you do not know what you are looking for. Like most decision-making, employee selection is fundamentally gut-feeling and this is the worst thing any leader can possibly do. While taking interviews most of the leaders become Antaryami (Immanent), they just decide if they like someone or not, and then they hire them. That's the most common way hiring happens in the world and makes a long-lasting impact on the organization. It leads to about a 50% hiring failure rate — that's based on about half a century worth of data on it.

I witnessed this firsthand when I was consulting one startup in the business of organic fruits and vegetables. One of my tasks was to help figure out why the sales team was underperforming. After interviewing various managers about their hiring criteria, I discovered a fatal flaw in their assessment process.

Mera Wala Pink (Only my preferred one)

It was the most successful campaign started by Asian Paints in the early nineties. Asian Paints wanted to convey that don't compromise on your choice and buy the exact colour you want. In the same way, many leaders also don't compromise while hiring, the only difference is the look for people who are like them, or at least they have similar habits/preferences or their life journey is the same. A lot of leaders feel more comfortable with people who are like them.

One of the people that I know working in the textile industry as Vice President was a big fan of Cricket. He was leading the company's cricket team as Captain and was participating in many corporate game events. Nothing wrong with it, but the problem was the HR department was instructed by him that if any candidate has cricket in the personal hobbies section of the resume should be given the topmost priority out of other candidates. If a candidate is found good in cricket, then it doesn't matter what position he/she has applied for or what skills they carry, the selection is confirmed.

Another example is one of the fast-growing telecommunication Company's head who always had a preference to select the candidate from his native.

It's okay that leaders can have a hunch as per their preference and convenience, but that should never become a substitute for evaluating and hiring for the right skill set required to achieve the organization's goal. The downside of this desire to create a company of clones is that it limits cultural diversity and diversity of thought and undermines innovation and creativity.

Extracurricular Activity

For many leaders selecting candidates for their team is an extracurricular activity. They do it when they are free or don't want to do another thing at that time. For many, interviewing the candidate is not rocket science, they can do it anytime. No preparation, pre-assessment or even reading the resume is also not required. Considering candidate selection as a secondary or additional activity impacts the leaders with **"Four A Syndrome"** (Articulate, Assertive, Attractive, and Affable) where they are assessing a candidate's presentation skills over business performance and substance.

For sure, we have all been there. Think back to your latest recruitment challenge that might have looked something like this. This unpreparedness leads to two common traps:

1. Resume Formatting Trap: As soon the leader sees the model resume which has the right amount of information, the font type and size are reader-friendly, there's lots of white space and a beautiful build-up. Well, a formatted resume becomes the eye-catching and most common assumption is how well organized that person is, and further selection starts with that biasing.

2. Date Trap: This is another big trap when the interview becomes the "date". The person sitting across is on his/her best behaviour. S/He does what I call the tell, sell, and swell:

- S/He tells what he thinks the leader wants to hear.
- S/He sells the best parts of his/her background.
- S/He tries to swell the leader's ego.

Does this mean the candidate is dishonest? Not always. Normally, people position themselves in the best light so their interview can go well and they can demonstrate that they are friendly, articulate, and speaks fluently and coherently. And most of the time actual skills required for the job go to the back burner, as a candidate is attractive, well dressed, and presentable, and build rapport quickly and easily with this trap.

This makes leaders more comfortable and they start asking easy questions (or goes in poor assessment) to get a home run.

Candidate selection is the first step of leadership. I don't advise people on creating the processes, having AI tools for assessment, because all this information is easily available. Tools and processes can assist leaders with the right data and assessment, but finally, leaders have to take the call.

But the game starts with how leaders are attracting the right talent. Do they have that magnet? How they are leaving the company's impression on the candidate's mind, because they are representing the company. Their brand name can only bring the candidate up to the interview room, but taking that right candidate to an office desk depends on the leader.

As a leader just think over it and ask yourself about your approach and practice of selecting the candidates to build a team.

- Is team building a priority for you?
- Do you focus on filling a position or building a team?
- Do you judge or you select?
- Do you go prepared to take an interview?
- Do you select by organizational requirements or personal preference?
- Is an interview an opportunity for you to showcase your knowledge?
- Does rejecting someone give you a sense of power?
- Do you seek what someone knows or dig to find what someone doesn't know?
- And finally, do you build a team or gather folks alike you?

"No one can whistle a symphony, It takes a whole orchestra to play it"

-Halford E. Luccock

2

Mil Gai To Manzil Nahi Mila To Rasta

LEADER WITHOUT VISION

"When leaders are working without any vision or hijacked someone else vision, if they achieve something it was the goal for them otherwise going with the flow"

I reached the office bit early from my usual time. One client was scheduled to visit our office and my presentation was still pending. So I thought to be early in the office to finish it with the help of some colleagues before starting the regular day. Just saw that Aashutosh was sitting in the office and looking very upset, although I was in a bit rush but thought to buzz him.

Aashutosh is one of the key members of our team with vast experience in consulting. He carries great acumen in solving complex business problems.

"Hey, Aashutosh you look upset buddy. What happened?"

"Nothing much Nikhil, *bus sir phodena ka man kar raha hai* (I am going nuts)."- Aashutosh.

"Buddy pehle mera presentation pura kar de, baad mai jo chahe kar lena (Buddy just finish my presentation first then do whatever you want.)".

"This is not good Boss, I never imagined that you will be so selfish, and more than me you are worried for a presentation." – Aashutosh winked at me.

I offered a coffee and said, *"To bhai chewing gum ki tarah kheech mat, bata kya hua* (Then don't stretch it, tell me what happened.)".

"Just now one of my friends called me and was looking to write a vision statement for his company and that too just over the call. What the crap this is, vision banana hai *bhajiye nahi*(Vision statement is to be created not the fritters recipe.)?"- Aashutosh.

"Nothing wrong in it Aashutosh, he is your friend and just looking for help.", now it's my time to wink on Aashutosh.

"That's not fair Nikhil, do you believe he is running a chain of physiotherapy centers across the bay area successfully for the last 4 years, earning good profits, and can ask such a question? I was expecting some level of business acumen from him. I am not able to visualize how he is running the business so far. What kind of leader he is?"- Aashutosh.

"I think now you are exaggerating it. Believe me, most of the businessmen are like this only. Let me correct you all businessmen are not leaders by default. Running a business and becoming a leader are two different things. It's good to have leadership skills for businessmen but not essential. People can run the business across life without having leadership quality.

So your friend is. What's a big deal, anyways why is he looking for a vision statement?"

"Out of the blue, some investors got interested in his physiotherapy centers and want to invest a good amount of money. They asked him to submit the business plan and they are emphasizing on the vision statement. He worked out the business plan but wanted me to design some good vision statement for him with which he can impress his investors." – Aashutosh.

"I told him that I don't know anything about his business, how he is driving, and where he wanted to take it. So how can I draft a vision statement for him? And to my surprise, he responded that he also doesn't know. But wanted me to do some magic with words to give him the vision statement." – Aashutosh.

"Then he must have given you the suggestion to search some company's website related to his business, then copy multiple vision statements and put them in a grinder and mix well to get some juice out of it."

"How do you know Nikhil, he asked me to see some of the statements and figure out them?" Now Aashutosh was laughing.

"That's the most common Jugaad leaders follow to develop a vision statement for their organization. I can say 80% of vision and mission statements are derived like this. There is a famous idiom in Hindi, *'Kaheen Kee EentKaheen Ka Roda, Bhaanumatee Ne KunabaJoda'.* Leaders become Bhanumati and pick some phrases from here and there to make their own vision statement." I said firmly.

Kiran was attentively listening to this conversation between me and Aashutosh and was keen to jump into the discussion. She recently came from India on 3 months assignment. We have a big team of consultants in India who are helping us to manage our Indian clients and also assisting in some assignments here in the USA, as well as in other countries. We are in the field of business consulting so our people need to be exposed to different countries, cultures, people, and organizations. This gives them not only the learning but also helps them to develop a different perspective to understand the client's problem by trying to fit in their shoes and suggest the best solution. Kiran is our rising star, always curious, eager to learn and the best part is, she raises the right and valid questions.

"Looks like you have something to share, Kiran", I looked at Kiran and waved her to be a part of the discussion.

"Yes correctly said Nikhil, I have seen many companies in India that are regressively following *Jugaad* practice to develop their vision and mission statements. In some of our assignments I have asked clients a few questions about their vision and mission, but they were unable to answer. I was like if you don't know about it how can you own it?" – Kiran.

"Actually to your surprise, Kiran, in most of the organizations, vision and mission statements are an important part of the office's interior design, corporate website, marketing brochures, and PowerPoint presentations. Once an organization reaches some sizable limit (in revenue or maybe in headcount) then the urge starts to have some *'Vision and Mission'* statement that can be a frame on walls so the employee can read and think that now they are working in some big organization, and the same aspiration can be conveyed to customers and partners".

"True, leaders are more passionate about the decoration of their vision and mission statement. They spend money and time to decide how to market it rather understand it."- Aashutosh.

"But why does a leader need a vision? What's the problem in copying from others, if someone is doing well then what's the problem in copying it. Besides that many leaders are running their business successfully without the vision too."- Kiran asked with full surprise.

"If you don't have a baby, are you going to abduct someone else's baby?"

"No, not at all, Nikhil"- while saying Kiran looked astonished and I can sense her inner voice what a disgusting question it is.

"But leaders do it knowingly or unknowingly. Vision is the leader's baby, they conceive it or it's a dream which they saw to transform, contribute and uplift people's life or society. So it cannot be copied from others because everyone is different, their belief and value system is different. Then how come their vision be the same."

"And I disagree with your point that many leaders run a successful business without the vision. Every leader has a vision, and it's a different aspect that they have shared it with others or not. I am against the businessmen turned in self-proclaimed leaders, no business can flourish without the leader having a vision and a business can grow multifold once it is shared and accepted by others."

"In other words, leadership is all about seeing and creating a brighter and better future. It's about inventing, innovating, creating, developing, improving, and transforming education, healthcare, business, government, technology, and every aspect of our lives and the world we live in."- Aashutosh added.

"I would say leaders without vision are wandering leaders, a rolling stone without the moss."

"hmm, you mean to say Nikhil, *Bin penade ka lota*(A leader without any foundation)"- Kiran said with a smile on her face. "I got it, and yes it's true that without vision no leader can drive, and it's a purpose for them and their organization."

"Yes, purpose helps them to be focused and to channelize their all energy and resources to achieve their dream. In life, everything is ready to distract you from your goals and others and your journey becomes *Mil Gai To Manzil Nahi Mila To Rasta* (If achieved it's a goal otherwise something is achieved)".

"But why it is important to share with others. Leaders know what they are supposed to do, others just have to follow their instruction." – Kiran.

"Great things in business are never done by one person, they are done by the team, together. The leader alone cannot achieve anything. They need people who believe in their vision and ready to work with them to achieve it."

"Kiran, vision cannot be achieved by just following the instruction or doing some task, first people have to believe in leader and then their vision. Unless people are not aligned with the vision of a leader or don't see their own goals are being achieved under the leadership or unable to visualize the value of their contribution, no vision can be achieved."

"I am trying to gulp that people have to believe in their leaders, and see whether their goals are being achieved or not, and so on. However, I believe many people don't have the maturity to understand such complexity and all these jargons. But still, I see people get attracted to leaders and their vision. How come?"- Kiran raised a question and her question was valid.

"I will answer your question but first, tell me why some people are leaders and some are followers."

"I know the theoretical answer but would prefer to listen from you Nikhil. Because I know you must have some deep definition otherwise you wouldn't ask such a simple thing."- Kiran.

"No Kiran, it's not like that." I laughed, and continued "Because the biggest characteristic of a leader is, they are the risk-takers, they risk their time, efforts, energy, money, even sometimes family to fulfill their vision."

"You might have heard about Martin Luthar King and his speech" I have a Dream". His vision was equality and freedom and he risked his entire life to fight for civil rights. Our Gandhi Ji saw the dream of freedom and took the risk to fight with the British Kingdom without any arms and ammunition. There are many other examples like John F. Kennedy had a vision for sending a man to the moon. Ronald Reagan saw the Berlin Wall come down before it crumbled. Steve Jobs imagined the iPod and iPhone long before the world was addicted to them. Abraham Lincoln envisioned a united America. Every leader has put up their life, career, the image on risk to achieve something which no one was envisioning it and people put their trust in those leaders."

"Now coming to the followers. Followers are people who don't want to take a risk or don't have the skill and capability to take the risk. So they look for protection or hope to get protected by their leaders. There may be cases when people may not understand the leader's vision thoroughly or can't understand them completely. But as long as a leader and their vision make people feel protected or make them hopeful about their future, they will trust them. In the professional world, protection and hope are about their job security, career growth, learning, earning, and work-life balance."

"Alignment comes when what leader is offering to protect or to instigate the hope that is matching with the follower's expectation from their protection and hopes. That's a reason it's important to share the vision with their followers."

"We all know about a lighthouse, it helps ships to navigate in the right direction. Similarly, vision works as a lighthouse of organization and provides the right direction to everyone, and also warns people to come back on track if they get deviated. It always reminds us where we are supposed to go, how far we are, and what is yet to be done to reach there. There may not be concrete strategies, well-defined plans but vision provides the path forward and keeps reminding the team where to focus and put all energy."

"It's correct that the leader sees the vision and his team believe in it. But everyone wants to contribute, to create value in whatever they are doing, wants a bright future, wants an accomplishment and vision gives them the direction and hopes that their desires will be fulfilled".

"But beware if the leader and the team are just thinking about the vision only, then sometimes it becomes the *Mungerilal ke haseen sapne*(A famous Indian television drama where the main character Mungerilal always kept daydreaming to take revenge on his boss and his father-in-law for their day to day harassment in his life) which never converts into reality. The vision should be supported by the proper road map with a measurable action plan. That's a reason leaders should always be equipped with a telescope and microscope. A telescope helps the leader and team to keep a focus on the big picture and a microscope helps to zero down on the small-small actions that are helping towards to reach the vision. If a leader has only the microscope then they might be working hard and putting in their efforts every day without knowing what progress they are making day by day to reach near to the vision in absence of the telescope. And on the other side, if a leader has only the telescope, they will just enjoy dreaming their vision without having any control over actions. The leader has to create a balance and should be resourceful to use a telescope and microscope appropriately. "

"I never thought that vision has such deep value and how it helps leaders and organizations to bring transformation Nikhil. An example of a telescope and microscope reminds me of the famous quote 'Vision without action is merely a dream. Action without vision just passes the time. Vision with action can change the world. But apart from the strategies and planning does vision impact other areas of business in the organization?" – Kiran.

"It impacts everywhere, it's the foundation of an organization. It works as a bible and keeps reminding people what they are supposed to do or not to do. For example, Walt Disney's vision is "To make people happy". Then whatever their team does whether it's a new theme/ride in an amusement park or a new cartoon character, it makes people happy."

"Another example is McDonald's, their vision is to give the world's best experience to customers in the quick-service restaurant category, whether it's an Indian or USA customer, they get the same seamless experience in their outlets. There are endless examples such as Starbucks, Microsoft, Apple."

"You shared a good point, but the kind of experience we get in McDonald's, Starbucks, or Disney doesn't it come due to the well-defined process? What Vision can do?"- Kiran.

"Ya, it looks that way. What the process is?" after a pause I continued "Process is nothing but well defined and tested steps to finish the work. Can all burger restaurants have the same process?".

"No, everyone has their way of working and based on that they define the process."-Kiran.

"Well said, 'their way' is nothing but comes from the vision. Again coming back to the McDonald example, they keep improving and making changes to fight with the competition, adding localized dish but whatever they do, they make sure that their customers are getting the great experience. Just because of this when you want to eat a burger, the first thing that comes to mind is McDonald's."

"Like Zappos' vision is to 'Deliver WOW', and to achieve this vision they have derived a system in place where they offer $2000 to quit at the end of the first week of training to new joiners. Because they know their vision cannot be achieved by non-committed average people. Zappos only wants people who are keen to deliver WOW to their customer – everyone else can take the money and go."

"Most call centers are set up by policies and so the actual person that's answering the phone can't do anything. But Zappos is different they don't have processes or policies which usually you may find in most of the call centers. Zappos doesn't value the processing of high call volumes, nor quick-time resolution. Nonetheless, each agent is expected to spend at least 80% of their time in customer-facing interactions. Whether this equates to 100 calls a day, or just 1, it doesn't matter – how long it takes to make each customer happy is time well spent for Zappos. You can see how Zappos has defined their process, system, and policies to achieve the organizational vision."

"So it's the vision which not only drives the process, system, policies but also influences all decisions."

"True, actually it makes everyone's life easy in an organization, people will always have clarity what they are supposed to do even if there is no well-defined process."- Kiran.

"I have another question, does it mean that vision is to estimate future realities and then to operate effectively within those parameters as well as save the organization from risk."- Kiran.

"Sometimes it looks like that but I would say the purpose of the vision is to create the future and it's not about mitigating the risk. Risk is inevitable and bound to happen whatever we do."

"Okay, what if the leader and their team together design the vision"- Kiran.

"This is the worst way to create the vision. Vision comes from the leader's philosophy, it's their dream, and people come and go. But it is leader who keeps moving ahead with that vision. Setting a vision is a leader's job that can't be delegated further. If multiple people are helping the leader to create, then everyone would be giving inputs based on their philosophy and preferences. It's an impractical thing to bring the common vision from the group because everyone wants their vision should be given priority. And how can one leader carry the surrogate vision? People can help the leader to chalk down the strategy and plan to achieve the vision. It's the leader who sets the vision and people who believe in it."

"Do you think it's a good way to make a catchy slogan to communicate the vision?"- Kiran.

"I don't see any problem whether you make it catchy or make a wall hanging or display site, as long as people understand it, believe it and they are fully aligned with it. Otherwise, it becomes the showpiece of your office interior and marketing material."

"Ya I agree, it's about how you want to communicate the vision but people should be aligned with it. But over a period, we tend to forget. How a leader can keep the vision alive, as they are already communicating in different ways?"- Kiran.

"Kiran, it's the most important thing for leaders to do, and communicating vision doesn't mean reiterating it in every meeting, making a part of the email signature, printed on walls. The most effective way of communicating vision is, it should reflect in the leader's behaviour, their decisions, their way of working, choices they made. Seeing is believing when people see their leader's conviction towards the vision they easily get aligned. Leaders should always seek a formal and informal way of communication to keep conveying their vision and philosophy."

"One of the people I know, who was working on a leadership position was always insisting to his people about the importance of communication. His expectation was, even if people are going out of the office for an hour they should inform him. But he never used to inform his team when he was not coming for a week. Although it's a very small example, tell me how people are going to believe his words. These little things become huge one day. One of the other leaders was always preaching to everyone in his team to be humble and respectful, but he never followed the same. He got easily out of control and forgot all his preaching when things are not as per his mood. So leader's character, behaviour and integrity make vision more relevant."

"What is the difference between mission and core values, as many people get confused between them including me?"- Kiran.

"The mission is the purpose, **Why do business exist, What leader is trying to achieve through Business.** The easiest way to look around what they are doing in day-to-day activities. The mission (purpose) is a supporting factor of a clear vision; if the vision is **Why/What** then the mission is **How.**"

"Core values are the **essence of the organization identity**– the principles, beliefs, or philosophy that leaders want to inculcate in organizational culture. It supports the vision of the organization, shapes the culture by reflecting its value. It impacts people's behaviour, their decisions, and how they react to challenges/situations. It becomes the guiding principle for people to make their choices and actions either consciously or unconsciously. This overall helps to build a great organizational culture."

"Could you please highlight the difference, I have understood but wanted to make sure."- Kiran.

"In my layman's understanding of vision is **Where you're going** then the mission is **How you will get where you want to be** and core values **guiding principle of the journey**.

"That's fantastic, Nikhil, I never thought vision has such a deeper meaning and how it is important for leaders and organizations to be driven by their vision if they wanted to become a part of any transformation. It's a base ingredient of a successful recipe for any organization. I would rather say vision can help the leaders to develop a strong and meaningful relationship with their team. They start sharing the same dream, which will automatically reduce any conflicts that arise in day-to-day working."

"Thank you, Kiran, for asking such great questions. Curiosity is the key to learning, I have a meeting in the next 10 minutes. Will catch you later."

Are you a visionary leader? Just ask these questions to yourself.

- Are you driven by the vision or do you go with the flow?
- Is your vision a combination of other's visions?
- Have you derived the vision from somewhere else or your dream and goals have derived it? Is it reflecting your passion?
- How much is the gap between your dream and vision statement?
- Do you really believe in your vision?
- How you have derived your vision?
- Does the process and policies of your organization reflect your vision?
- Do you have a roadmap to achieve your vision? If yes how frequently you are revisiting your plan and keep it updated based on the market changes.
- What efforts do you make to keep your vision alive and reinstate it with your team?
- Is your team also following the same vision?
- Do your team members believe that they will be able to achieve their vision by following yours?
- Have you ever done one-to-one meetings with your team members to know their vision and identified whether both visions are matching with each other or not?

"The only thing worse than being blind is having sight but no vision"

-Helen Keller

3

Aham Brahmasmi

TRUST DEFICIT IN LEADERSHIP

"When the leader starts feeling 'I am the God' and expect people to forget everything and just trust in them, so they can manipulate their trust as they want"

Hey, Nikhil, Sethi again called.

"Hmmm", I just nodded my head without looking at Monika. I just wanted to avoid her, as I was busy working on a very big proposal.

"This is the third time he called me and now asking me for your mobile number, tell me what I should say". Monika said to me. She is a Front Desk Executive in our office, working for 5 years with us. Now it looks like without my firm answer she is not going to leave the cabin. Someone named Mr. Sethi is making a constant follow-up to award an assignment to us and right now we don't have any bandwidth to take up anything.

"Make an excuse to him, you know better how to handle such folks. At this moment I am not interested in taking any assignment, you know that we are working on a very big proposal and that's the priority we have right now." I said, and actually, I just wanted to wind up the discussion.

"I don't think any excuse will work now, all exhausted", she cunningly looked at me. "And, Nikhil I have already explained to Mr.Sethi that you are not available for the next 2-3 months, and if required he can consult 'Aashutosh' but he denied. He is very clear that he wanted to meet you, I would say just talk to him once and it would be better if you tell him about your unavailability. I believe Sethi thinks that I am not conveying his messages to you and now he is suspicious about me. You know I don't like this at all, so you need to take a call." Monika was speaking in full flow and was not in the mood to get interrupted. "Okay, okay I got it, you can fix the meeting next week maybe on Thursday or Friday".

"Thanks, sir, for saving me". Monika said and left the room. I could read from Monika's face that she was frustrated with the constant follow-up of Sethi (*"a prospect or lead"* so-called in sales) and she didn't want to lie to anymore.

Anyway, I just wanted to focus again on finishing the proposal. But now the mobile started ringing, it's Mohan. Mohan is my friend and we were colleagues, now working as Regional Head with a retail chain.

"Hey, Mohan!!! Whats up man, good to connect with you after a long time. How is everything?".

"All good Nikhil, yes bit busy these days. We are expanding in the bay area and just opened a new store in Oakland" - Mohan.

"That's great, is there anything urgent as I am in the middle of something?" I wanted to talk with him, as we got connected after a long time but the proposal was banging on my head.

"No problem Nikhil, *tu continue kar* (You can continue). I have one request if you can accommodate it"- Mohan.

"Ya, sure anytime Mohan".

"One of my friends, Vimal Sethi is trying to reach you. He is my school buddy and he needs your advice badly. " – Mohan.

"Oh, ya this fellow has contacted our office and I was busy with some important work so couldn't talk with him. Anyway, now I will reach out on priority. Sorry about it."

"No issues Nikhil, I know how busy you are."- Mohan.

"Mohan! Can you give me some background about him"?

"Ya sure, He is running RPO (Recruitment Process Outsourcing) in India, pretty good clientele in the US. But facing a lot of bumps in his business since last year. So I thought who can be better than you to advise him. The good part is, at this moment he is in the bay area on a business trip so can meet you personally." – Mohan.

"Thanks for sharing, I will work out something with Mr.Sethi. *Chal,* catch you later, and let's also plan one family get-together some weekend".

"Ya, would love to do that. Take care, Bye"- Mohan.

Monika fixed the meeting, and Vimal Sethi is coming to the office on Wednesday's second half. My company is providing consulting to startups and mid-sized organizations for leadership development. Our work is not to create processes, business templates, provide online video training, etc, I literally hate this model. In my view every organization is different, people are different, and their values are different than how come one consulting model fits all organizations. "One size doesn't fit all", actually "Not at all". Our model is understanding the client's unique challenges, their pattern, actions, and instead of changing them or implementing some readymade model; fine-tune their model itself with some level of leadership transformation.

• • • • • •

Monika told me that Mr.Sethi has arrived and is waiting for me in the conference room. I asked Monika to order *"Samosa"* (Indian Snacks) from Ajanta Restaurant, if someone is coming from India or any of my Indian friends or client is coming to the office, *"Samosa"* from Ajanta is fixed for snacks. Ajanta is one of the famous Indian restaurants in the Bay Area and is near our office. Sometimes when I do the introspection I feel, this gesture that I offer, is this for me, because of my immense love for *Samosa* or for someone else.

"Welcome, Vimal, Good to see you here at our office. I am so sorry about the delay in this meeting, truly speaking I was stuck with some other priority."

"Oh, no-no Nikhil. I can understand it, the only reason I was chasing your office as next weekend I am flying back to India. So I was eager to meet you. I heard a lot about you not only from Mohan but also from many people in our circle. I am following you on LinkedIn, and amazed with your views on leadership and management"- Vimal

"Thanks, Vimal for kind words. I didn't know you were in the States, frankly speaking in any of my conversations with Monika, our front desk executive to whom you were talking didn't say that you are here. I think there was some communication gap. "

"Hmmm, now I also realized that I haven't communicated to your office clearly about it. Someone said correctly, Assumption is the mother of all screw-ups."- Vimal.

"Please help yourself Vimal, with coffee or Tea. We have also a *Desi* Chai pre-mix if you are missing it and *Samosa* is on the way".

"Nikhil is sab ki kya jarorat thi (Why you are doing these formalities Nikhil?). I am good, but missing the chai. Would love to have it"- Vimal.

"Great, let's discuss for which you are here. Mohan told me that you are facing some issues and looking for some advice".

"Yes, that's true. Let me give you some background."- Vimal.

"I am based in Indore and running the company named 'Recruitment Mantra', dealing in recruitment process outsourcing. Entire BackOffice is setup in Indore with the capacity of a hundred plus people and sales offices in various major locations such as Bhopal, Delhi, Noida, Gurgaon, Mumbai, Ahmedabad, mainly operating in the western and central part of India. Apart from this, I have a good clientele in California with some tech startups, for them, I am running the night shift in India. We are managing the recruitment operation of many renowned banks and IT companies."-Vimal.

"I had started this business in 2009 with one shared desk in the business center and slowly and gradually reached up to this level. Up to 2017, we were small, and things were manageable. But post that we grew up, expanded our business and suddenly a lot of problems started pouring and solving one problem resulted in another problem and it kept going. That doesn't mean we are not able to run the show, we are. But it's just managing the things, we are not growing. And most of the issues are people-oriented, my team is having challenges with each other and that is impacting each area of business including the client. And I had to intervene everywhere to solve the issue. This chokes my time, energy, and focus, and I am not able to do what I am supposed to do."-Vimal.

"I hired highly talented, experienced, and skilled people, I thought they can solve issues, somehow that didn't work. Not only this I tried many other things, like sponsoring my team for the training program, offering rewards, incentives and it worked for some time, and then again things were on the same track. I even personally started giving them the training, investing my own time, but no improvements. I feel I am doing a lot for my team but the team doesn't have the value for it." Vimal was flawlessly speaking but the way he was telling it was not giving me a good sense. It's like he is doing *'Ehasaan'* (favor) for his team and they are not able to meet his expectations. I always dislike this attitude of leaders.

"Nikhil, they are taking me, the company, and my offerings for granted. They don't have respect for me. They don't feel obliged what I am doing for them, you tell me who is giving such things for an employee in India. I am keeping a friendly relationship with my employees and I have an open-door policy, they can come any time to meet me. Even I am trying to help them with their problems. So I am looking forward to your quick advice, how to deal with this situation." – Vimal.

"I hear you Vimal."

"Then tell me what the solution is, I am very hopeful that I will be flying back with some solution."-Vimal.

I never like people who create unnecessary pressure and set unrealistic expectations and that's the reason I usually avoid direct meetings with first-timers. Just doing it because of Mohan's recommendations. People think consulting is like selling *"Aloo-Pyaz* (Potato-Onion)", *"bhav bola aur tol diya* (Just negotiate the price and buy it)".

"Vimal, I am not a magician, you said and I listened. But before suggesting you anything I need to dig further. You have your side of the story I need to listen to what your team thinks?"

"That means you are not trusting my words Nikhil and want to verify with my team."- Vimal.

"No Vimal, if I start suggesting you based on whatever you have said now, it would be reacting to one part of the problem. Please understand your team is also equally contributing to your organization's growth. Whether they are meeting your expectation or not, it's a different story. But they are contributing. If you are interested to address the issues, then we need to work together and it will take some time. Unfortunately, there is no quick remedy. "

"Hmmm, how much time it will take Nikhil?"-Vimal

"At least 3 months, and further I can say once we diagnose the issues. One of my consultants will visit your office and try to meet all important stakeholders, he will conduct various interviews, surveys, workshops, and feedback sessions to understand the root cause. Because many times when we see the problem, we try to solve the problem based on its symptoms without understanding its root cause. We will need complete support from you, as you may feel uncomfortable or awkward during this process."

"No that's fine, I am a very open person. Let's do that"- Vimal.

"Great my team will explain to you the nitty-gritty and once the proposal is signed we will start the work."

"Thanks, Nikhil for your time and listening to me. I am excited about this transformation."-Vimal.

• • • • • •

A few days later Monika informed us that Vimal has signed the contract and we are all set to start the assignment with Vimal. Aashutosh, our senior-most consultant is assigned to Vimal as there is constant pressure from Mohan to give special attention otherwise I could have sent someone from the India office. Aashutosh visited the Vimal's office in Indore stayed over there for three weeks and did extensive research to understand the root cause of the problem as stated by the Vimal.

Aashutosh is back from India after conducting the discovery workshop in Vimal's company. Although I was in constant touch with Aashutosh when he was there, but I was excited to know more in detail. As per the process, Aashutosh is supposed to present his findings in form of stories with an internal panel including me. And our presentation includes the cases and based on those cases we brainstorm for the root cause of the issue and later to a solution. So sharing the different cases learned at Vimal's company.

"I am presenting two major cases of Vimal's company which I have discovered during the discovery phase there are other 12 cases which you can read from the discovery document. But I believe you will be able to figure out what's going in Vimal Sethi Company and what needs to be fixed."- Aashutosh.

Everyone nodded the head and given the go-ahead to share the case studies.

Mai Mark Zuckerberg banna chahata hoon
(I want to become Mark Zuckerberg, founder of Facebook)

Vimal called an urgent meeting in his cabin and asked everyone to be present. In a couple of minutes, everyone was rushing towards the Vimal's cabin. As the seating arrangement of Vimal's cabin is limited some were able to sit and some were standing, but everyone had a question mark on their faces about what happened? Is something good or bad? Because Vimal is known for his tantrums in the office. Keeping fingers crossed all were looking at Vimal's face.

Finally, Vimal broke the silence and said I have good news to share. Everyone was relieved oh, something is good, then let it be whatever it comes. Vimal continued, Today I have invested in one product, developed by one of my known friend and past colleague. It's an internet startup and developing a job portal. It is in the primary stage, so I got a stake at a very good rate and by looking at our recruitment business this would help us significantly in our operation. Today we are paying the premium cost to all job portals and it sucks our margin. They are charging us per user, so having our portal will save a lot of money and along with the pride of having our product.

Everyone in the room was neutral, they were neither happy nor sad. Because many times they have seen the impulsive decision of Vimal and that cost on the company's growth resulting in an individual's growth adversely. *"Sir, kya aapne product ko evaluate kiya hai* (Sir, have you evaluated the product?)." Meghraj, Head of IT said after gaining a lot of courage to speak in front of Vimal. Now courage is extended to Operation head Sahil, he also added *"Vimal Sir, ek baar team se to check karwa lete* (Vimal sir at least you could have discussed with the team)."

Vimal didn't like the questions, but he was in a good mood so he just ignored them. He was on cloud 9 with the feeling of standing in line with Mark Zuckerberg, Larry Page after investing and owning the product. He said, "Don't worry. Mark my words, people will remember this day and it will create a history."

No one was happy, especially the core team was feeling they don't have any value in the organization, at least Vimal could have taken them in confidence before taking such an important decision when this decision is going to impact the organization, their involvement was necessary. But nothing happened, and everyone had to become *"Charan-Bhat"* (In the past people who were praising the king was known as 'Charan-Bhat') and praised the decision of Vimal.

In the next couple of days, Vimal's company started using the new job portal, which was full of issues and challenges. Recruiters were facing the problem in their day to day activities, they were not able to search candidates, post the job requirement and many more things which they were doing easily previously with the other well-known job portal. All these issues were resulting in the delay in getting recruitment work done, and subsequently increasing customer dissatisfaction. This was impacting everyone's work performance, leading to work-related stress. Sahil, the operation head took the initiative and reached out to the development team of the job portal where Vimal has invested. To the surprise, he didn't get the proper response and was asked to have patience as these are the teething problem which is expected with any new products and he was also advised to wait for the next release of the portal to get these problem resolved.

Sahil thought to discuss with Vimal before these challenges go beyond control, and coincidently at the same time, Vimal called him on his EPABX extension *"Idhar Aana"* (come here), and the phone gets disconnected. Sahil immediately rushes to Vimal's cabin and was articulating in his mind how he is going to present all the issues. But as soon as he entered Vimal's cabin, he listened to the rough voice.

"Tum logo ko kam karna nahi aata kya (You people don't know how to work?)?"- Vimal.

And Sahil was shocked, what happened? He humbly asked, *"Sir, Kya Hua* (Sir, What happened anything wrong?)".

"Kya hua kya (What the hell), who asked you to talk with the development team. You and your team don't know how to work and you are complaining to others."- Vimal.

"But Sir, there are serious problems with the job portal. My team is not able to work, their productivity is getting down due to the issues. They are reluctant to work with the new system."- Sahil.

"You people don't understand the Product, and what the product development is, you are just cribbing and giving the excuses."-Vimal.

Sahil in his mind, "Ya true, we don't need to understand the product and we are not interested too. We are coming here to test someone's product or to provide recruitment services for our clients?"

Vimal continued speaking, "I am giving you all the new opportunity but you want to remain the same in the old fashion. I know how to get this fixed."

Sahil just listened to the word "fixed", and thought "Aha, finally we will get some fix." He said, "What is the fix, sir?"

"I am going to discontinue the subscription of all standard job portals. When there is no option you and your team have to use the new portal."- Vimal.

"What???" Sahil was about to say but he controlled and said: "Sir, this will impact badly to our operation, productivity and team morale".

"I am ready to take this heat, our focus is to make this product successful. This my vision for **my company**."- Vimal.

Sahil was speechless, he was thinking he didn't know when the company's vision got changed from recruitment to the product development company, and are we crazy to put the running business at stake just to make other product (which is still grooming) successful. Can't we have a proper strategy to take this product up if it is so important for an organization instead of impacting all business? There were many questions in mind, but no point in discussing with Vimal, as he is so adamant and not in the mood of listening to anything negative about his new baby.

Another thing which makes him highly upset is when Vimal said my *company*, so far he always listened from the Vimal that it is our *company* and he and all other team members made endless efforts making anything possible. When did this transition happen from our *company* to my *company?* Sahil was not able to digest it.

Later Sahil and the team saw more drastic decisions, like the discontinuation of the standard job portal, and everyone was forced to use the new portal. Many people left the job, as they were not able to perform and the recruitment business works on the incentive when someone gets recruited, recruiters get incentives. Due to the ongoing issues recruitment count went down hence incentives too. People started feeling they are becoming guinea-pig for the new product and it was not just about the incentives, recruiters were not seeing the value addition in their career growth as it was not improving their skill required for recruitment.

Vimal continues to solve the problem but in a different direction, he hired the software developers to fix those issues and that made the whole scenario worse. Now instead of having the team of recruiters, there are new teams that are testing the job portal and another one who is fixing the issues of the portal. Means Recruitment Company turned in a software development company.

In the next couple of months when this innovation started hampering the cash flow, Vimal started feeling the real heat. The excitement of becoming Mark Zuckerburg started going away, but it was very difficult to admit in front of everyone. The company has already lost some of the key accounts. Now time to take some hard steps, but unfortunately that step created another case of disaster.

Ye meri company hai, mujhe ise bachana hai (This is my company, I have to save it)

It's like Vimal woke up after a long sleep when everything was already about to collapse despite having warnings and suggestions from his team members. The experiment of becoming a product company miserably failed, now Vimal is facing problem in paying salaries and manage the day to day expenditure. Salary increments were already due, he was extending from the last two months with the promise of having more attractive increments because the product was supposed to save money. But nothing happened rather product sucked the cash reserve of the company.

Anyways, the D-Day has come, Vimal called Sahil and other department heads for an urgent meeting.

"You all know what the present situation of the company is."- Vimal

"Yes Sir, we understand."- Someone replied in the low voice, and other team members just nodded their heads.

"I am holding off the product initiative and subscribing again to the standard job portal to resolve the team challenges for day-to-day work."- Vimal.

Everyone was so relieved and happy about this announcement. "Thank you sir", everyone said in one voice. Everyone was about to leave.

"Hold it, I have something to say. **It's my company and I have to save it,** I can't bear such a large team with this cash flow. So we have to fire the team and bring down the salaries to 40%."- Vimal.

Everyone was shocked, the entire world was collapsing in the eyes of Sahil and other team members. No one was able to speak up, it looked like their voice choked. Sahil was speaking in his mind, "Sir I have been telling you for 4 months, that things are not going right with this new venture and you were not listening. Not only me, everyone was saying the same thing. Even all the people have indicated negatively in monthly feedback about your initiative. You could have talked to us before starting this project, I have been working in this company for the last 9 years and I always wished and worked towards the company's growth. But you didn't, you never trusted your people. Now when things are messed again you are not trusting us and just giving the decision."

"Any comments", Vimal broke the silence and continued "I know it's a tough thing but no choice is left. But don't worry your job is safe."

"Yes sir, we got it but trying to digest this. How we are going to tell people about this news, we are already in a critical situation and struggling to sustain in business. With this news, everyone will be shattered. I am afraid of how we are going to run the show post such a level of firing."-Sahil.

"To kya mai sab ko ghar se khilaon, jab tha kabhi kuch mana kiya? Abi muje company bachani hai" (I never said no for anything when the company was doing good but in such a tough time do you expect me to pay from my pocket. I have to save the company right now.)-Vimal.

Negativity and discouragement were rising in the room, and a simultaneously inner battle of Sahil's mind was continuing **"You are right sir, whenever we had a pressure of work, there were tough targets to achieve, and you always said to people this is your company. Work like a CEO, you are not an employee. Now it is your company and you have to save it.** What will happen to those people who trusted the company when things are not going right for the last 4-5 months? They were working hard and putting endless efforts to run the company. People believe in your words when you said that I am postponing the salary increments for good and you will have a good raise after a couple of months. Everyone trusted you. You don't have any value, because now it's your company".

"How much time we have to plan for this."- Kamal, HR head said to Vimal. In the end, it's his responsibility to execute.

"What time do you need? Do it today. I can't continue"- Vimal.

"Sir it would be very difficult, this will create chaos. People will be highly disappointed and angry, it may have some legal repercussions. We need to see from all aspects."-Kamal spoke while looking at Sahil to get his affirmation.

"Ye business aise hi nahi chalaya, ye legal vegal kuch nahi hota (I am not afraid about the legal aspect, I know how to run the business.). I will manage it."-Vimal.

"Okay Sir, how you want to filter the people to retain and ask to leave?"-Kamal.

"You figure out, I am only concerned about the salary reduction to 40% and to make sure current work should be uninterrupted. Go and figure out, I would say fire highly paid people they are the costly one. "- Vimal.

"Sir, sorry to say they are not costly, they are experienced people and getting salary based on their experience and competencies. Based on the present workload and requirement we need such people in our team. Otherwise, it will be very difficult. " Now it's a Sahil turn, he was afraid without the good team how things will work.

"Apart from this, Vimal sir there are other commitments to our employees, we have to honour. I believe that they will be intact. "- Kamal.

"What commitments?"-Vimal.

"There is variable pay due from the last 3 quarters, incentives are pending. Besides that, we have to pay a three-month salary to all employees to whom we are going to fire."- Kamal.

"No-no, I don't have any money, nothing will be paid. Except for this month salary."- Vimal

No one had the capacity and authority to stretch the discussion with Vimal. Everyone surrendered and did whatever was asked. It made a huge negative impact on company images, the remaining people started leaving due to insecurity and they were facing difficulty to hire new talent. First, 6-7 months went in the experiment of a new venture and the next one year went in the recovery of that experiment.

"I am done with two important incidents of Vimal's company. Rest you can read from the document, but this is sufficient enough to understand how much he is doing for his company and people and why he is facing a lot of issues.", Aashutosh said.

"I got it. It's a very common issue especially in India with the mid-size or small companies or I would say most of the companies."- That's my immediate response but not the conclusion.

I further added "It's nothing but a trust issue with the leaders where they don't feel or needed to properly communicate the real reason of their decisions. As they believe as a leader it's not their responsibility to make people understand, rather people have to align with them to understand their decisions."

"That's it? Over a month-long visit to India we have zero down on this?" – John just reacted to my response, he is a management trainee and joined our company three months back.

"Yes if you have observed both the stories, Vimal didn't trust his team to take the opinion before taking such big decisions. His team could have given good inputs."

"Nikhil, there could be some other reason than the trust."-John

"I understand what you are thinking, but believe me, this is the only reason. Trust is the foundation of any relationship, it's an emotional bond that gets developed between leaders and their team through repeated interaction and provides comfort and stability. If the employee and employer don't trust each other they can't achieve growth. They both must come together to achieve something, the employer shows the dream and the employee believes in it, then they work together to achieve that dream. During this journey, they go through a lot of ups and downs, challenges, where trust works as a foundation to keep them aligned. The absence of trust separates their path and if paths are different they can't reach a common goal. Ultimately if the purpose of coming together gets dissolved then they might be working together but not towards growth. That's what Vimal was saying when he was here in our office that they are not growing."

"Interesting Nikhil, I never knew that trust is such an important ingredient in a business. But I believe it's vice versa, employee trusting employer and in return employer trusting employee. So it has to be from both sides."- John.

"Yes, you are right, John. When an employee agrees to work with any company, he already trusts the company, its leaders, and its vision. Now it's the time of the leader to have trust in them. No one comes to the workplace to disrupt the work, it's the employer's primary responsibility to trust them that they are coming to contribute to their goal."

"Then why is there is an absence of trust, Nikhil? The leader or employer is giving salaries and investing in the employee then why they are not going to trust. What option is left with them apart from not trusting their team?" – John.

"Working together doesn't mean that you are trusting each other, people can also work without trusting each other. Is the leader hiring or building the team to get some work done or to achieve some goal? If the objective is to get some work done, this goes into the transactional relationship where they both look at each other to finish the transaction. But if you want to build something together, it cannot be achieved without trust. I hope you got the answer, John, we are also doing many activities where we are paying money to get things done. No question comes about trust if they are skilled enough to finish that work (transaction)."

"Now I am getting more clarity, Nikhil, the spectrum of trust is much wider than what I thought. Tell me why leaders don't trust their teammates? Are they not trustworthy?"- John.

"No that's not the case if they are not trustworthy no leader or employer will keep them. Let's not go into the people's integrity issue John, keep the focus on a trust issue with leadership. As I said people have already shown the trust in a leader when they aligned their path with them, it's about the leaders how they are going to trust their people."

"If you see in both the cases as explained by Aashutosh, it's clear that Vimal did not trust his teammates. He had not shared anything with them before announcing his decree."

"Why are you saying decree? And Vimal might have the apprehension that his team may not agree with his decision that could be the reason for not sharing."- John.

"No John, trust comes with confidence. Based on the events and details shared by Aashutosh, Vimal himself was not confident about his decision, as he didn't have any exposure to product development. Investing in an IT startup was more wishful thinking, a hidden desire to be known and become popular as an investor. That's a reason he didn't share with team members."

"What's wrong with it Nikhil? Leaders take risks, it's a quality and how can you say he was not confident?"-John.

"John, confidence comes when you work with facts. I agree that leaders take risks and they have to take them. But there are always some calculations, facts, and figures which become the foundation of your risk-taking capacity. If any leader is just taking the risk on gut feeling then it's a pure-play gamble, with the probability of getting a win or lose 50-50%. That's what the Vimal's case is".

"But what would have happened even if he shared?"-John.

"It makes a huge difference, if he had shared, then his team would have bombarded him with a lot of questions, provided some facts and figures about their capacity, organization readiness to accept this new change, alignment of organization resources, and much more. All these things could have helped Vimal to make a better decision."

"If the core team was aligned then subsequently they could have aligned the team members down the line. The team could be responsive and accountable if they were part of that decision, in the above case the team became reactive. Because the decision was imposed on them, so even if there was something good with that change, the team was not able to see that. Finally when the organization's condition became worse and Vimal had asked people to leave, then apprehension of the core team converted into reality. They were like we were saying since the beginning and Vimal sir was not listening to us and it was bound to happen. When the leader and his team have a different belief system, they are not going to trust each other instead they will be suspicious of each other's activities."

"This is giving me a clear picture of, why it is important for leaders to trust their team members and if there is no trust that means there is no team just a group of people doing some transactional activities for each other. But why doesn't a leader trust their team?"- John.

"I would like to add something here, Nikhil."-Aashutosh said as he was actively listening to the conversation.

"Would love to hear from you Aashutosh, please go ahead." – I said.

"Based on my experience as I have seen in all my past case studies when leaders carry some hidden agenda or something else in mind then they don't trust people. Because they have an apprehension of being exposed to their real motive and purpose to people."-Aashutosh

"Sorry to interrupt Aashutosh, hiding is nothing but the personal agenda. It's an individual choice whether to share the personal agenda with others or not? I don't see anything wrong in it."-John.

"No John hidden agenda is a different thing, it's an agenda where leaders are driving the people by showing some other agenda or goal but actually, they want to fulfill something else. Like most politicians do it. In this case, Vimal shows the agenda of having one other line of business by owning the product, but his hidden agenda was becoming famous as Mark Zuckerberg." Aashutosh continued speaking in adding more reason.

Jo hum boltehain wo hum karte nahi aur jo karte hain wo bolte nahin (What we speak we don't do it and what we do we don't speak it)

As I was saying many leaders have their personal goals and objectives of running the business and there is no harm in having it. But the problem is if those goals are not creating any value to their people, customers, partners, and society who are directly or indirectly getting impacted, can't be shared publicly. So they must articulate some fabricated goals to share with everyone.

This double-faced personality of leaders brought down the 'less' or 'no' transparency with their team members resulting in 'low' or 'no' trust. One of our clients who was working as Internal Sales Head in a Pharma Company and his wish was to have his passport stamped with maximum countries visits. So he was making unnecessary trips to fulfill his wish but without bringing any results. Not only this, he was seizing the opportunity of others who could bring the business. For others, it appeared that his goal was to 'close more sales' whereas he was working towards the goal of 'visiting more and more countries'. So even if his marketing team was giving good leads but many times he was just ignoring them because those leads belonged to countries that were not on his wish list. At the same time, he was also not recommending another team member to handle those leads because of two reasons. The first reason, if others close the leads then his chances would be reduced to travel in the future and the second reason if others start traveling then the traveling budget would be shared with others and that will impact his further plan of visiting new countries.

Hoshiyaar, Yahan ke hum hai Rajkumar (Kindly Attention I am the Prince here)

Many leaders are arrogant by nature, they treat themselves like king or prince and they don't believe in being respectful with their teammates, as they believe being humble is a weak character and they always want to show how strong they are. People are afraid and avoid interacting with arrogant leaders, which leads to less exchanging of ideas and thoughts between them. This doesn't allow to development of trust between both of them, as trust comes from knowing each other's background, capabilities, area of interest, like and dislike.

Chacha Chaudhary (Uncle Chaudhary)

Many of you know about *Chacha Chowdhary* (an Indian comic book character by Pran), his mind works faster than the computer. Many leaders are like *Chachaji*, the smartest people of that company. They feel it's a compulsion for them to be smart, hence they cannot be ignored, challenged, or questioned. If someone dares, they are immediately criticized. This self-illusion develops a strong sense in a leader that trusting their people is not required, as they are the smartest ones and don't need anyone else.

I and Aashutosh continued to explain to the group what the impact is when a leader lacks in trusting its people.

Lack of Agility in Business

In today's world agility is the key to success in business, a distrusting environment brings down the speed of the work wheel. Because leaders don't trust their people, they start trusting on unnecessary processes, review cycles, a long chain of approvals/permissions of small-small things, the business of CC/BCC of emails, etc. All these things consume a lot of time, energy, and efforts of people, and diverts the focus from growing business and customers to follow the system which got generated as their leaders don't have the trust in them. Hence the time in responding to the market, business, and customers increases significantly and the agility required for business takes the back seat.

Here my intent is not to say that processes and systems are bad, they are good but you should not forget it's the people who transformed the business, not the system and process. Process and system are to help people to work with agility, not to lose their working agility.

Increase in Operational Expenses

As I mentioned above, a distrusting environment requires a lot of processes, systems, log keeping, audit & monitoring including additional staff to manage all this. This costs an additional operational expense for an organization to maintain.

No Innovation and Improvements

When a leader doesn't trust their people, he starts challenging and questioning them if they are coming up with an idea for the improvement or some innovation that doesn't suit the leader's hidden goals or their supremacy. Slowly and gradually people stop coming up with ideas as no one wants to be punished if they are not being appreciated.

In today's world companies cannot afford to stay afloat if they do not embrace innovation and change. Because, it directly impacts the organization's growth, helps in staying ahead in the market with competitors, improves efficiency, and most importantly it keeps business, people, and their skills relevant to the market.

Increases Dependency on the Leader

When leaders don't trust their people, they have to involve everywhere starting from how much tea/coffee is being consumed at the pantry to what the core team is supposed to do. This behaviour of a leader impacts the organization's culture because the culture is derived from the way a leader behaves and leads. This makes the organization's environment, where no one takes responsibility and looks towards the leaders. And even if they try to take it, there is always a fear that a leader might scold them.

This makes the leader do all activities which are supposed to be done by others. Then they are not focused on their responsibilities of taking an organization to the next level, which ultimately hampers the growth of the organization. Beware!! **'Growth'** of an organization and **'manage'** to run the organization are two different aspects.

Decreases Employee Morale

As employees are not being trusted by the leaders, it makes a huge impact on their morale. They don't feel empowered to perform their duties, as their actions, decisions, and even intentions are being challenged and doubted. This decreases their interest in their role to play, and they just perform the task assigned to them.

Needless to say, all these things heavily impacted the customer experience and business, as in an untrustworthy environment people are unable to perform with their best as they are focused on pleasing the leaders rather than long-term values and commitments.

Trust forms the basis of all relationships and interactions. It is just as important in professional relationships as it is with personal ones. A leader who develops a trustworthy environment can easily stand in a tough time whether it occurs due to the competition or any market crises or maybe in COVID like a pandemic. When a leader is transparent with people, they tend to respect, care and listen to them carefully.

According to the Harvard Business Review when leaders create a trusted environment people experience 74% less stress, 50% higher productivity, 106% more energy at work, 13% fewer sick days, 76% more engagement, 29% more satisfaction in their lives, and 40% less burnout.

People, when trusted by their leaders, are more energetic at work, collaborate better with them, and stay with them longer than people working with a leader who doesn't trust. This makes people happier, fulfilled, empowered and all these factors fuel stronger performance.

Leaders trusting their people is a non-negotiable thing, the bottom line is leaders can't expect their people to perform if they are unable to trust them.

As a leader do you trust your people? Just ask these questions to yourself.

- Are your own goals or hidden agenda interfering with your people's performance and your commitment to your team's success?
- How often do you think of firing a person who is not aligned with 'you'?
- How often do you give your "two cents" advice even when it is not being asked?
- Do you prefer to get updates or information directly from the responsible person or through your informers/secret agents?
- How often do you react to someone without listening their side, just based on the inputs provided by your informers/secret agents?
- Do you hold grudges with your people if they challenge you and then do the settlement when your time comes?
- How often do you yell at people and make them feel to doubt their capacities?
- Do you listen to your people and seek their ideas, suggestions, and opinion?
- Do you collaborate with your people while making an important decision?
- Do you set and communicate expectations with your people consistently?
- Do you stick to your words and commitment even in tough times?
- How often do you change your statement and views?
- Do you treat everyone with the same dignity and respect without being biased, judgemental, or favoritism?
- Do you set a good example and conduct yourself in a manner consistent with the mission, vision, and values of the organization?

"Over time, I have come to this simple definition of leadership. Leadership is getting results in a way that inspires trust"

-Stephen Covey

4

Achchhe Din Aaenge

IMPORTANCE OF PROMISE IN LEADERSHIP

"When the leader doesn't keep promises they make and take pride in breaking them"

It is almost dawn and the sleep seems far far away. I am not able to sleep or even put my mind to rest from the troubles. Yes, I am anxious. At an extent that I have never felt so confused, distressed, and lost even in my most struggling days.

A week after is the first anniversary of my consulting company. I should be happy. It is a dream come true that I have completed the first year. All the hard work has started to pay off and the uncertainties of the future have started to settle down. The progress we are making as a start-up is in the direction we thought of. I should be proud of what I have achieved in the first year, a good competent hard-working team which is the most important ingredient for a startup to succeed, a handsome pipeline of prospects, and the team getting good exposure. I am glad to find great people to work with me. There is every reason for me to be happy but I am not because it's the time when I have to fulfill the promises I have made to the team and I find myself unable to fulfill that and this thought is killing me.

The company started well and we were able to establish ourselves in the market quickly. People have started to recognize us. My team has done so much hard work throughout the year and now it started to pay off but not in monetary terms. The future looks promising, our sales pipeline is healthy but that's the future, reality is we are still a startup. We are still in our cradle, our balance sheet is still not booking profits, on the contrary, the truth is I am still providing the company with my savings. I don't say that we are in bad shape but I am not in the position to give the well-deserving reward to my team and there is every reason that they would be expecting it. Why wouldn't they, after so much effort they have put throughout the year and it is because of that I can say with full confidence that the future is bright.

The thought which is killing me is, as a leader what if I was not able to give the promised increments, is it OK? Is it OK for a leader not to fulfill the promises they made?

I was still in deep thought when the sun came up and Avantika woke up.

"Nikhil! You haven't slept all night?"

"*Naaa*(No)", I replied.

"What happened?" she was worried, her eyes were wide open from surprise and fear "Is everything alright?"

"Ya I am fine, don't worry. Give me a strong cup of hot coffee. I badly need that." I replied and tried to avoid the worries from my face.

"Sure," she said with a smile and came to my side of the bed and put her palm on my forehead. She was worried that I might be sick.

"I am alright, dear" and took her hand in my hand removing it from my forehead.

"Tell me what is bothering you, will you?" that's how Avantika always tricks me to share with her everything. She asks, never commands.

"Yes, it's something with the office," I replied.

"I have never seen you troubled by anything so much. I have been noticing it for a few weeks." Avantika was concerned. "As you know I never interfere in your office work but I think you should share, maybe that would help. Think about it meanwhile I will get you your strong coffee cup." she winked at me to cheer me up.

She returned pretty soon with two cups of coffee and now we were sitting in our balcony watching the rising sun and sipping our coffee.

"Avantika what happens when promises aren't kept? Even if one has a very good reason for breaking promises." It came out of my mouth as my mind was struggling the whole night.

"There will be consequences nevertheless. "She replied with a blank face without looking at me.

"Oh man" she is straight I thought. She continued "I am assuming it's a promise made to your team."

I nodded in despair. She continued "Can I ask you a question?"

I nodded again.

"Will you break a promise made to your family?" Avantika.

"No! Never, but it's different... It's business." I tried to plead.

"Do you call your team your family?" Avantika is now in an affirmative tone.

"Yes but .... That's different. They are not you or kids." I started getting irritated.

"If it is different, then you should stop using that in the office with your team," she said with a cold voice and stood up from her chair. I held her hand and asked her to sit again. I need her advice badly right now more than ever, I need someone to hear me out.

"I don't want to break a promise by choice but the reality is I can't fulfill it right now." I tried to convince her.

She was looking into my eyes and was able to see the pain and truth in them. "If this is the case, let's see what we can do in this situation. If you have failed to keep the promises the best you can do is to have a closure conversation with the person or the team whichever is your case."

"And what that would be?" I asked.

"In a closure conversation, you will first acknowledge that you failed to keep your promises. Secondly, acknowledge that you understand that it has impacted the person or the team with whom you made the promise. Lastly and most importantly you apologize for the trouble, pain, disappointment, setbacks you have caused. And finally, offer your help to cope with whatever you can do." Avantika replied.

I was expecting a similar response from Avantika and what else you can do in such a situation, "You know Avantika that's actually kind of what I have thought. I have planned to confront the team and deal with the situation with direct communication. I will address the issue and communicate why I am not able to fulfill my promises and will ask for their understanding. They will understand, why wouldn't they, I will explain the whole scenario to them."

Then I firmly said with some level of proud "What else I can do. It is what it is and I am transparent with them. At least I am doing that much. How many leaders have that much courage to communicate with such transparency? At Least I am better than them. That's what great leaders do."

"Yes, that's what great leaders do," Avantika murmured.

"What have you said?" Looks like Avantika was sarcastic in response and she smiled "Nothing Nikhil."

I can sense the relief in my head. Now I have a solution to it. I can see that it's OK if sometimes circumstances don't permit you to keep your promises but you can show good leadership too. The team will definitely understand. "Oh gosh, it's such a relief." I thought the conversation is now ending.

"But there will be a cost to it," Avantika said while standing from the chair and went to the kitchen.

"On sec.... Cost? What cost? Wait a minute." I followed her to the kitchen.

"See Nikhil having a close conversation is not the solution. It doesn't make anything right or better. You as a leader breaking your promise is a double-edged sword. It will not only have an adverse impact on the team but on you as a leader as well." Avantika opened another conversation.

"Closure conversation is damage control, Nikhil, It will not make everything better but it can surely help." Avantika.

The relief was gone as quickly as it came. Oh! this is killing me. "You were talking about some costs. No doubt there is a cost of breaking promises, Yes, but what cost?" I was furious.

"It will surely damage your relationship and your reputation as a leader. When promises are broken or people are misled, the bond of trust is breached. Doesn't a broken promise make the team feel violated or cheated? Think about it." Avantika.

She continued, "Nikhil you are a leader of your team and your word is your bond. You can't afford to be casual about the promise you make. Every promise made by you as a leader, you are putting your honor on the line. When you break a promise you have to face the consequences and the impact can be deep and enduring."

"But I don't have a choice," I responded.

"Yes but be prepared, the team will be upset and they have all the right to be upset." Avantika.

"I will explain it to them. Why they will be upset, they will understand." I was not understanding what Avantika is trying to make me understand but I strongly believe in being transparent is the toughest thing and leaders hardly dare to do it.

"Because they have counted on you, they have given their hundred percent, they have played their part. But the leader doesn't understand this. The leader breaks the promise and when the team shows their displeasure they feel bad." Avantika.

"I will share the reason with them."

"Leaders lose credibility even when they have a very good reason or excuse. Credibility suffers from every broken promise. The team loses trust in you as a leader. Even when a leader shouts his lungs out that he is trustworthy, the team will not share his opinion.. The leader will lose affinity. The team will stop respecting them or at least not in the same way they used to do. Like it or not the leader cannot have the same affection back." Avantika replied and I can sense she is trying to give me the visibility beyond by card of being transparent.

I felt upset again. My head started aching again. I went back to the balcony and sank into the chair. Avantika came and sat closer to me.

"Nikhil I know it's troubling you. The salary revisions in the company are coming. I can understand your trouble that you have made promises to the team of yearly increments, bonus and you are afraid you might not keep your promise." Avantika.

I nodded without looking at her.

"I want you to keep your promise. Yes, Nikhil. One thing you should understand is that sometimes leaders get away with breaking promises but later they make a habit of it. Whenever there are slightest of unfavorable conditions or circumstances they don't hesitate in dropping their promise and make excuses and still consider themselves as leaders. They might be but in their own world. I don't want you to be that kind of leader no matter how much you convince yourself that it will not happen again." Avantika.

"Then what shall I do. It is not feasible right now to do the increments."

"Nikhil it's not only the increment but the reward of their hard work. Aren't they working hard to make your dream a success? Haven't they aligned their dreams and their success with yours?" Avantika.

"Yes they have, No doubt without their contribution we couldn't have come that far." Avantika.

"Then remember that a leader is always a provider if it is a family or an organization. If you can't do a handsome one then do a modest one but you should reward your team" Avantika.

"Yes but that will be very difficult too."

"Ok I will help you with my savings, but consider it as a loan only. I will be wanting that back with interest, strictly professional." She was smiling and my troubles started to fade away with her smile.

"Quick question Avantika, from where did you get such insight on this topic." I was curious to know.

"Nikhil, the word 'Promise', that's a heavy-duty word and it shouldn't be used lightly. I have learned a long time ago in parenting." Avantika.

"Parenting?? How come?" I was surprised.

"Yes, everyone who becomes a parent probably gets into the situation where we made a somewhat casual or flippant 'promise'—Sure, Jiya, I promise we'll go to the beach next weekend—only for it to not happen. What is the first thing the child says when you don't deliver? But you promised!", Avantika.

"Whether it's a Starbucks that makes a promise by printing on their coffee mugs 'Our Barista Promise Love your beverage or let us know, 'We'll always make it right' or a promise made by Dominos that they deliver in 30 minutes. These companies keep their promises whatever it comes to, for example, if you don't like your drink then Starbucks will remake it or make you a different one, dominos will not charge you if they are late. They won't make the excuse. So, what does this have to do with leadership? Well, it's pretty simple: What is your leadership promise? What is it your people can expect from you or count on you to do no matter what?" Avantika was speaking in a flow and I was amazed that I have such hidden talent in my home.

She continued, "The point is Nikhil, you need to be clear on your leadership promise(s) because even if you aren't, your team members have ascribed them to you based on your past behavior. You are setting yourself up to break trust with your followers if their perception of your leadership promise doesn't align with your own. With this, my time is up, and have to go out. But not forget to send me a consulting fee." She left for some work.

I was thinking that in what kind of illusion I am living, I was always carrying the pride of being transparent and blunt in communication but these are just words and if words are not empowered with action, then they are only fake promises. When I was in need that everyone should work day and night to accelerate the growth of my company, I was telling to everyone that "It's your company" and when some tough time came for me my statement got changed to "It's my company and I have to save it". How selfish I was. What is the fault of my team, they trusted me, they believed in my words, and with that promise, they went beyond the limit to take the organization to the next level. And in return, I am just delivering the so-called transparent words that "Whatever promise I made was fake and will not be fulfilled." I was completely wrong.

It's the leaders who keep their promises that can boost performance, enhance their credibility, inspire and engage the team, and build trust; those who break promises to constituents lose credibility and trust. Although most leaders understand the importance of keeping promises, few see them as maintaining them, and hence often break them and suffer the sad consequences. And promises are not just limited to offering about salary, bonus or perks, there are more important and unsaid promises which every team member expect from their leaders.

- First promise: Set the right direction and create a meaningful goal.
- Second promise: Engage all team members and hold them accountable for performance.
- Third promise: Ensure that processes and systems facilitate focus and execution.
- Fourth promise: Lead effectively and maintain relationships of trust to achieve desired results.

When the first promise is broken, the organization fails to be competitive and thus declines. When the second promise is broken, the team underperforms, turnover decreases, competition wins market share, and the organization declines. When the third promise is broken, all types of resources and time are wasted; the organization becomes mired in a culture of resentment and hopelessness, and ultimately declines. If the fourth promise is broken then there is no probability of meeting the first three promises.

Most importantly when leaders sitting on top don't keep their promise, then people down the line follow the same. It becomes the culture of the organization and not only team members of the organization suffer even their customers and vendors also take the hit. People frequently say "I will get back to you by tomorrow", do they mean it? No, most of the people take it very casually. It's a 'promise' they made but unfortunately, they will not respond unless being followed. And this unconscious bias doesn't stay unnoticed or unspoken about. Ultimately it delivers as an experience of the organization whenever someone interacts with any of the channels be it employee, customer, or vendor. The organization not only loses its credibility, trust, and accountability, but it also has strategic risks including losing key talent, a poor employer reputation, customer losses, and eventually poor morale all across.

As a leader be careful of every promise, big or small, you make to anyone, big or small. It is your word. It is you. As someone had once said, "A promise is a promise." Period. Don't make promises if you honestly are not sure about keeping them. It breaks hearts. And kills your credibility at all times. Remember the cliché: Better to under-promise and over-deliver. You will then always stay a leader with a promise — honest and genuine, just check out some of the questions for introspection.

- Do you understand the importance of keeping promises with the team as a leader?
- Have you faced a situation where you find it difficult to keep your promises to your team?
- Have you ever had to choose between making a team understand or keeping your promise?
- Have you ever found yourself in a situation where you have to take a toll to keep your promises to the team?
- Have you faced the repercussions of breaking a promise with the team and don't know how to deal with them?
- In what realms of your leadership are you willing to have people call you out if you don't deliver?
- What are your core values and is keeping the promise part of it?

"A highly credible leader under promises and over delivers"

-Stephen Covey

5

Chit Bhi Meri Patt Bhi Meri

INSECURITIES OF LEADERS

"When a leader wants to keep the upper hand in any situation"

It seems like it happened yesterday, so far yet so fresh in memories. Whenever some memories of college come by, they leave a smile, I think this happens with everyone. I shook my head to come in present and was reaching to my mobile to check for messages or emails at the very moment it rang.

I took it out, there were three missed calls from *"Sethji"*. I was a bit surprised that what happened *Sethji* is calling. I feed his number as *Sethji* a long time back in sheer humor, in the northern part of India business owners are being called *Sethji* out of respect. And most of the owners feel good about it as it separates them from the *"Aam Admi"* (Common Man) class to the elite class. The new generation of owners doesn't like to be called *Sethji* but they are happy to be treated like *Sethji.*

He was my ex-boss from India who was calling, and like any other owners, he also feels delighted being *Sethji.* Although, I never called him *Sethji* but always treated him like that.

Indian business culture is all about *'Sir', 'Saheb', 'Sethji'* and *'Salute'.* Indian philosophy and moral values emphasize on treating every human being with dignity and empathy. In reality, we are prone to over-stepping these professed moral boundaries. Due to it, people in authority believe that reverence is their fundamental right and returning the same to others is not necessary.

In the western world, we use words such as 'Sir' and 'Madam' fewer times a year than we do every day in India. I believe these words were originated from the British colonial times to establish a relationship between master and their people and have gone away in the West as those relationships no longer exist. But, for us in India, the hierarchy between human beings is an important component of our social system.

Calling the seniors or owners by name is not limited to the businesses. Under patriarchy, women in India are not allowed to take the name of their husbands and elders. Similarly, people in the lower caste are not allowed to call upper caste people by their name. So, our Indian culture is effortlessly married into *'Sir', 'Saheb', 'Sethji'* and *'Madam'* to add honor to people. We have inherited this in our culture and habits and created layers everywhere in society. Even the small organizations quickly develop the hierarchy for interaction. Just visit any shop and you may find one *'Sethji'* (owner) and others like *'Ramu', 'Chotu', 'Bhola'* are on the lower side of the hierarchy. People in a lower position keep groveling, wait in front of their seniors for hours and try their best to appease the *'Sethji'* or people in the upper hierarchy.

Although time has changed, many organizations are trying to get rid away from this culture. But in reality, *'Sir', 'Saheb', 'Sethji'* become uncomfortable with advocacy of abolishing preferential culture. They always claim we are equal, it's a flat structure, no one is boss, you are the CEO of company and blah-blah-blah but time to time they also remind you that they are the 'king' and you are just an employee of their kingdom.

'Sir' or 'Sethji' fix meetings and keep their people waiting without any regret, they suffer from the anxiety attack to discover if someone other is talented down the line. They want to become polite but fears of not being taken seriously by the people from the low hierarchy, speaking in a loud voice, humiliating others, unpredictable behaviour gives the sense of power to *'Sethji'.*

Organizations have a well-defined democratic process, responsible people in decision-making structures, but all powers are in the hand of the *'Sethji'* irrespective of the outcome given by the so-called democratic process. This culture doesn't encourage 'risk-taking' and 'innovation', which is a mantra of success in the modern world. The organization's goals become secondary and less important as the focus shift to make *'Sethji'* happy. Even facts & figures get failed in front of *'Sethji's'* mood. This makes the organization culture where time, efforts, and resources are put together to cheer *'Sethji'* which results in making organizations weak and towering the *'Sethji'.*

I believe being courteous or humble is not a bad thing but that should not be limited to the seniors or elders, it should be for everyone irrespective of position or seniority. The other viewpoint in the English language, which has taken over as a working language in most of the official places in India, the pronoun for addressing someone, with respect, has been missing. "You" is the word that is used within the converses to address the other person and there is no way, in English grammar, you can identify the difference between the persons in conversation. For example, you can use "How are you" for your 4 years old son and 90-year-old grandpa as well. The only difference is the voice tone, which expresses the concern within the question.

In India, we have a variety of languages and all of these have different pronouns as well as verb forms for addressing the elders (read it, elders, by age, by position, by relation). We find it difficult to address elders by their first name (It took almost a year for me to address one of my colleagues, who is in his mid-60s, by his name, here in the USA, where calling Sir is a Knighthood).

So to overcome all these shyness, doubts, hurdles, and the inability to address by name, we must use Sir for the elderly just to show a gesture of respect. Something like, "How are you sir" when addressing my team lead, who is in his late 50s, and also while addressing one of my friend's grandfather (common language was English between us).

However, everything has its pros and cons, *'Sir/Sethji/Saheb/Madam'* went beyond respect and people started using it to keep them in a different class. The point here is not about whether to call Sir or Madam or calling everyone by their name. The real issue is are you calling them out of respect or by force (hiddenly or openly) to be accompanied by exaggerated bows, cringing gestures, and looking down to avoid eye contact. If junior cannot connect to the seniors/ leaders of the organization at the professional level, then I call it workplace discrimination which is the outcome of *'Sir/Sethji/Saheb/ Madam'.* This leads to low self-esteem, lower confidence, bowing, and flattering rather than face-to-face professional communication. We are so indulged in this culture that once our Prime Minister Narendra

Modi called Barack Obama by his first name during the former US President's visit to India in 2015, which raised eyebrows at the time.

No, I'm not stereotyping, but in contemporary India, though more workplaces are modernized, there is a lack of liberty in the boss-subordinate relationship which affects the free-flow of communication in the organization, because our way of addressing creates a mentality of someone being superior, the other being inferior, and that's why subordinate cannot openly disagree with the boss.

I was indulged in thoughts and suddenly the phone started ringing. It's *Sethji* calling back,

"Hello Sir, sorry missed your call." I use to call him Sir, not *Sethji,* from my side it was only to convey respect.

"No issues Nikhil, I have called you early in the morning. I hope I haven't disturbed you. "

"Are Sir kya baat karte hain aap, for you any time. Bataiye kaise yaad kiya. (Sir why you are saying this, for you, I am available any time. Tell me how I can help you.)" I replied in a full formal manner.

"Nothing specific just got to know that you are coming to India, so I called you, and please Nikhil don't call me Sir I always keep telling you but you never listened," *Sethji* replied.

Yes, he always told me that but I never believed him. Somewhere I am convinced that he feels good when I call him sir. Then why say no if he likes it? That's why he is *Sethji,* I giggled within but kept the tone firm and polite of my voice. I strongly believe in *"Achchha dikhana aur achchha sunana kisee ko bura nahin lagata, to achchha dikhaate rahiye aur achchha sunaate rahiye* (Who doesn't want to look good or be praised, so keep telling good things to people and make them feel good)."

"Yes Sir that's true, I will be there next week."

"Actually Nikhil, I want you to meet me once you are here in India." Still, my *Sethji* doesn't want to meet me, he wants me to meet him. Although on one side he says don't call me Sir, but his behaviour won't allow you to forget that you are talking to Sir.

"Sir, how can I say no to you. I will definitely meet you." I generally don't talk to everyone like this but *Sethji* always likes an extra spoon of sugar. However, I don't have any compulsion but there is no harm to maintaining the status quo in some of the relationships.

"Great!! I knew you will say yes and don't forget to bring Avantika. I hope she is doing great", *Sethji* replied.

But I was wondering why he wants to meet me, usually, he won't meet any person without any reason. So I asked, "Sir is there anything specific?"

"Yes, I am planning to expand the business hence working on a couple of strategies. So wanted to discuss this with you. Although I am quite confident that it will work but thought that you are coming here so would be good to listen to your thoughts. *Bhai kuchh bhee bolo seekhe to yaheen se ho* (whatever you say, but you have learned from here)." Finally, *Sethji* has given the verdict that I am nothing and whatever I am today is just because of him and his company, and still, he wants my advice. That's why he is *Sethji.*

"Okay Sir, *Sab aapaka hee to diya hai* (Sir everything is yours)". Once again I just increased the bits of sugar.

"Good, see you then."

I remember it didn't end well when we decided to part ways. Of course, there was no fight or heated argument but there were some major differences of opinion that led me to leave *Sethji* and his kingdom. Everything was not that way when I joined *Sethji* and his organization.

Memory lane took me to the day when I met first-time *Sethji* at a coffee house in Mumbai. It was supposed to be a casual meet so I was in casual jeans and a tee which was my favorite attire since college. As a punctual kid, I was on time and waiting for the other person as always. Punctuality is good but the only challenge is that there is no one to appreciate it.

After twenty minutes or so Mr. Biyani a.k.a. *Sethji* came. He was the CEO of a good and stable FMCG organization having a reputation of its own. Our meeting was set up by a friend of mine who has worked with Mr. Biyani in the past. He called me asking would you mind meeting my ex-boss. Why would I? So I agreed. I did a bit of research on him and his organization and found it quite impressive. Though the organization was not growing but maintaining a stable profitable stature which was not bad at all.

I remember our meeting started with a very formal introduction. We started to chat about current economics some topics from here and there and then gradually we started to mutually open up about what we do and what we want to do. To be more specific, Mr. Biyani was very keen to know about my work experience and what are my future ambitions which I shared very openly with him.

I shared, from the very start, I happen to be a very innovative person with some new ideas of doing things and always challenging the status quo. He seemed very impressed at that time and then he shared the current challenges he is facing in his organization. How badly he wants to grow at a much higher pace and how much deep understanding he possesses of his field. But somehow he is not able to go to the next orbit and is looking for people who can help him to achieve his mission.

His words were music to my ears. That's exactly what I was looking for throughout my journey. I was delighted to know his inclination towards new ideas and giving freedom to the team. That's the feeling I had that time. Mr.Biyani proposed me to join him as COO of his company which I accepted without much hesitation. Truly speaking I was on cloud nine.

And my journey started with his company and Mr.Biyani and also started the story of how Mr.Biyani gradually became *"Sethji"*.

• • • • • •

My first day in the organization was very cool, Mr. Biyani introduced me to key people of the organization. Soon I understood the traits of their business and started to work on some very intuitive proposals. I was very eager to present those to Mr. Biyani. They were bold in the sense that on a couple of occasions I challenged the ongoing strategies and practices and proposed the necessary corrections. I was pretty much sure that Mr. Biyani would love it and jump with joy after my presentation.

One fine day when all the key stakeholders of the company were there and I made the presentation. I proposed some reforms and new innovative strategies. I was curious whether my proposal would be liked by all or will be rejected, but to my surprise, the response was very cold. Ya cold. People didn't respond or react but were busier to read Mr.Biyani that what his response is. Mr. Biyani was also in deep thoughts and that was understandable to me but what about other guys. Say something good, bad, ugly, anything I was crying out loud inside me. Anyway, the meeting ended. Nothing was said. Mr.Biyani just said, "Meet me in my chamber".

"*Ahhh Yahi to chahiye tha...baaki ki kis ko padi thi* (This is what I wanted, who cares about others if the boss is interested)", that was the thought kicked in my mind. I very enthusiastically entered the chamber of Mr. Biyani. He looked serious and it was very hard for me to deduce whether he liked it or not. I believe there was no question of not liking it, not because I have made it very perfect but it was why I have brought to the company. If there were some corrections to be done I was open to it.

Mr. Biyani pointed to the chair, he wanted me to sit. I didn't like the way he did that but I sat, all the enthusiasm died all of sudden as someone has opened the lid of the soda bottle with an opener and phssssssssssss.

"You should have discussed with me first," Mr. Biyani said.

I didn't get what he was saying and before I speak he continued "Before presenting any new idea in the board meeting just discuss with me in advance."

"Is it that you didn't like my proposal?" I collected all courage and asked.

"No-no it's very good *bas ek baar pehle discuss kar liya karo aage se* (Discuss with me in advance before moving ahead)" Mr. Biyani replied and he kept on saying why it is good to share with him in advance otherwise everything was good and how much hard work I must have done and so forth, but the only thing I was hearing was to discuss with him first.

Only I can have all the Best Ideas

For the first time, I got a slight idea that it was Mr. Biyani's insecurities that were talking. Insecurity forces leaders to ensure that all the best ideas flow from them or at least through them. So they can claim the credit. Such insecure leaders are afraid of the people who are more talented than them.

An insecure leader will stop taking input from their team because he feels as if this lets people challenge their authority. But they forget team's work better when they feel as if they can speak up freely. There is a better chance of improving the team's performance when leaders aren't the only person coming up with good ideas. And in the case of their ideas leads to wrong decisions such leaders are not willing to explain what went wrong because it gives people a chance to criticize them. They think being less open will reduce the chance of anyone criticizing them.

This insecurity force people to recognize and appreciate their leaders as all new ideas are coming from them or endorsed by them only which makes the leader happier and believer of how bright they are. But ultimately it's a loss for the organization as it builds the culture that the best ideas can come only from the leader which is never the case. Although it makes leaders happy as so-called innovative ideas are coming from them or through them, people start talking about the leaders and that makes them happier.

Like one startup which was in its early stage of local grocery vendor listing on the website and trying to establish its business model. It was in early 2000 so many vendors were not keen to get enrolled with them. All of a sudden, the founder decided to publish the book of vendor listing with their rating. The way it was presented by the founders, other team members were forced to say "What an idea Sir Ji" and the focus was shifted from online to offline to publish the book. Web-Developers become the field agent to collect the data and for the next couple of months, everyone was putting their best to make their leader successful. But the result was a disaster as vendors were unhappy with their rating published, they were like what is your credibility to rate us. All efforts went into the vein. This is how the leader keeps the organization and their people's future at the stake just to prove their ideas are best and everyone and everything suffers as a result.

I know it All

Still, I continued to propose and pursue my proposals, ideas, and strategies. But Mr. Biyani though liked them all but never took any efforts to initiate. The organization required some bold decisions to be made as need of the hour, market, and business. I waited and waited but Mr. Biyani was always in procrastination mode or sometimes skipped communication and never took any action and I wondered why and the result was the same insecurity of his, no matter if it might take down the business.

Insecure leaders are frightened of coming across as insignificant or incompetent, so they overcompensate by pretending they know it all. They claim to be the champion of the business they are into and no one knows better than them and it is always claimed in words repeatedly without fail in front of the team. They rarely ask questions--and when they do, they rarely wait for the answer.

Insecure leaders assume all key assignments or anything which would give attention to the person completing them. They are careful not to give others the spotlight. They tend to control information–everything goes through them first.

Unwilling to take Challenges

But I kept a firm head and kept on working hard. Made some fruitful changes in my department. Soon my work was visible in the organization and I started getting appreciation from peers and my subordinates. And I think that was the last nail on my working relationship with Mr. Biyani. He started ignoring me, giving me a tough time in management meetings with irrelevant questions. I started feeling suffocated. But why, I did everything for the betterment of the organization. My every action is intended towards the growth of the organization. Then why these questions, that puzzled me. I closely looked at the core team of the organization and soon everything was clear to me.

We had a big-size back-office team and there were times when the team was sitting idle without any work. Some team members were enjoying being idle and many were concerned. And at the same time, there were some areas where people carrying the additional workload. I thought if we can align people having less workload with people carrying more work then it can create a balance. But the biggest challenge was who is going to ask everyone daily about their workload status, even if they inform their supervisors most of the time they were unable to inform others if free people can be utilized. We were using one software collaboration tool to update the work status, share updates and announcements. I asked everyone if they are free to just announce using the tool that they are free and willing to accommodate any suitable work. It made a significant impact and we were able to manage the workload of people. Everyone has taken this on a positive note, but I was wrong.

One day Mr. Biyani called me and his response was like what is the nonsense system you have made, Nikhil. I was not shocked as by that time I was habitual that my every constructive move is questionable. I gently asked, "Sir, what is the problem with it, we can utilize the people's free time to manage the workload."

"But it's damaging company image in front of the employee." Mr. Biyani. I was like what????

"People are announcing that they are free, that means they don't have any work. This gives an impression that the organization is unable to generate sufficient work, people will build a wrong impression about the organization. It's a simple math Nikhil." Mr. Biyani was looking at me and trying to make me feel in front of others that I am a fool and don't have a basic understanding. As usual, I had to surrender to take back the initiative.

Every initiative has its pros and cons, leaders have to see the wider picture and evaluate what tactical and strategic benefit they are getting out of any initiative. Another perspective of my initiative was that we were bringing transparency in the environment, and if there is an imbalance in workload then it is being managed. Top of that it was by the people, where people are saying that they are available to take the additional workload. So no chance of feeling the force to do the work. My view was a win-win situation.

When leaders are insecure, they don't like to take risks because they lack confidence in their ability to succeed. And if such a situation arises they become defensive or try to avoid any sort of communication. That doesn't mean that Mr. Biyani was not a passionate man but as an insecure leader he was more concerned about his passion rather than how his team's functioning, about how he was presented rather than how well the mission is being met.

The insecure leader flares his or her insecurity when ideas or decisions they make are challenged in any way. They remain protective of their position or performance. They are constantly looking over their shoulder expecting someone to question them or their authority.

Insecure leaders fear not being liked, so they often ignore the most difficult or awkward situations. They talk behind people's back rather confronting them. They are likely to say one thing to one person and something else to another – depending on what is popular at the time.

Secretly threatened by Great Talent

Later on, it became evident that the biggest blockage in the company's growth was the insecurities of Mr. Biyani as a leader. Some incidents happened thereafter which gave my thoughts more conviction. A few days later an old employee resigned as he got a good opportunity elsewhere. When Mr.Biyani came to know that, he became very angry and focused on the faults of the person leaving. I wonder why suddenly Mr. Biyani is changing his perception of that person. But then I realized insecure leaders see any employee departure as a poor reflection on their leadership.

You can Grow but only under Me

Slowly and gradually I realized that why there is a talent crunch in the organization. Mr. Biyani never hired a smarter person than him or by mistake, if someone gets hired or emerged more intelligent than him then he is either fired or forced to resign by hook or by crook. Because it is difficult to keep smart people under control and that it becomes a threat to Mr. Biyani that they may develop their independent identity within the organization. He always wanted that people should grow, but on his terms and mercy. Independent and strong personalities may not fulfill his "yes sir" need and may question his decisions and way of working. Such things were considered as intolerance in the organization. He always wanted that people should acknowledge his blessing and guidance on their success.

Makes Everything a Joke

One huge sign of an insecure leader, in my experience, is they make a joke about everything. Again, they don't want to handle the hard stuff – and want to be liked – so joking is often a coping mechanism used to divert attention from the issues they don't want to face. When people laugh, it gives a false sense of being liked to the insecure leader.

Mr. Biyani believed that by making a joke or laugh out loud at any serious matter or discussion he can divert the attention or can dilute the situation. But nothing was the case, in every such instance either he was losing the trust or people very getting annoyed. There were people hired as sales trainees and apart from the stipend they were promised a bonus if they achieved some target. Although Mr. Biyani was a *'Kanjoos Seth'* (A Stingy Owner) who never believed in paying an additional penny even if he's getting a good return and was always looking for an opportunity to eat up the hard earn share of others, agrees to pay bonus with a belief that trainees won't be able to achieve the target. But the world doesn't work the way he thought and trainees achieved the target and claimed their bonus. It was an utter shock for Mr. Biyani, instead of being happy and feeling proud that his team achieved the desired target, he was under the stress that now he had to pay the bonus. HR and Account Department reminded multiple times about the committed payment, but he was always trying to ignore it. One day all trainees entered his cabin to get the status of their payment. Mr. Biyani looked at everyone and said "I ate it" and then laughed like a king "ha-ha-ha". Now all trainees were in shock by seeing such a cruel joke. Out of respect, they didn't say anything but I can understand what feeling they carried.

Everything is in the Title

Mr. Biyani was very concerned and always making sure that no one is calling him by name, he used to consider it disrespectful. Once someone said that the world is changing and now people in senior positions refrain from calling them, Sir or Madam. He became very defensive and said whatever it comes but preferred to call him 'Sir'. The point here is not about Sir or Madam but his mind of keeping himself in an elite class.

An insecure leader tends to have a title or position. It does not matter what the position or title refers to, rather that they have something next to their name. They often see themselves as uniquely qualified for their position and mention that when talking with others.

Overly concerned about Personal Appearance

While this is not always the case, some insecure leaders are never far from a mirror. They are overly conscious of their clothing or hairstyle. Afraid of not being in style or wanting to be accepted as hip or cool, they are constantly looking for the latest fashion trends or attempting to be cutting edge with the gadgets they carry.

One of my colleagues in an organization was leading a department. His focus was always on how good-looking he is and if you visit him for any work, first 15-20 minutes one has to listen about his knowledge on latest brands, what he bought recently, which expensive wine he recently tasted, etc. There is nothing wrong with personal grooming and being stylish, but if leaders try to influence people with it rather than influencing them with their work it's insecurity.

• • • • • •

I always wanted to have a detailed discussion with Mr. Biyani about the current trends and future possibilities but to my surprise, he only listened and never asked any questions about what I said. His response was fixed "I will think and let you know". But that day never came into my life. That was strange to me but again it was the insecurity that was on the driving seat.

I can now clearly see that insecure leaders see people as working for them, not with them. They feel jealous when someone in their team receives public affirmation, and they are not mentioned. When they're insecure, they work hard to gain respect for themselves, sometimes even by belittling others to put themselves ahead. They have "yes" people around them and guard against anyone who displays leadership potential. They hand out titles only to those they believe will never question their authority. That's what was exactly happening in this organization.

My work started to get micromanaged by him, as he was very insecure and liked to control everything, even though I was doing what I am supposed to do. That time I decided to move on. I joined him with big dreams and high hopes. This was a classic example of an organization that had very high potential but was struggling because of an insecure leader.

Though the experience was not good with the organization, I have learned a very important lesson of professional life. "Insecurity though always shows up in a person's life. It can possibly be disguised, but it can't be hidden." I was looking forward to working with a leader, not a *Sethji* anymore.

Just answer these questions to know if you are leading with insecurities.

- Are you eager to find the mistakes of your team members and condemning them openly?
- Are you reprimanding team members publicly and believe that making an example of an employee will encourage the rest of the team to do better?
- Do you have the answer to everything and want everyone to know it?
- Do you try to ignore the important question or situation which is uncomfortable for you?
- Do you review team member's work on minutiae, take projects out of people's hands, and simply make them feel useless at every turn?
- Do you think that your team members are always thinking about you and your moves?
- Do you avoid working with new people?
- Do you feel threatened in hiring people who are more capable than you?
- Do you think people are avoiding you?
- Do you take advice from your team?
- Do you encourage feedback?
- Do you refuse to explain your decision to your team?
- Do you explain to your team how to do their job?
- Do you get angry when people quit?
- Do you blame others?
- Are you rude to your team when they commit mistakes?

"Insecure leaders use others to make themselves appear great"

-Jeremy Caris

6

Kaamchor Hi Makhan Chor

LEADERS PRACTISING FAVOURITISM

"When a leader creates cheerleader to make them happy"

Some assignments are tricky, but on the surface, when you start working it looks pretty straightforward and you feel that you will be done in no time. But it becomes like an onion, layer by layer things keep opening, and then what you get is different from the surface.

I worked on such an assignment, on prima facia I thought it's just a mistrust between the leaders but when I dig it, the case was entirely different. One company had approached us to evaluate some of its leadership profiles. The company was in the business of providing data analytics and business intelligence services mostly to the Asian continent. The company was founded by two college friends 11-12 years ago and one of the friends has approached me for a personal meeting. At that time I was in India for some assignment, also there were few personal things to attend to. When you visit India, there is always something on a personal end to look upon. Even if there is nothing, I smartly create so that I can stay a bit more in India.

"Here is Mr. Sudeep", Monica opens the door and introduces the gentlemen.

"Hey, Sudeep welcome, a pleasure to see you here!!!"

"Hello, Nikhil, same here. I am glad to meet you, I have heard a lot about you. I like your views on leadership which you regularly share on LinkedIn. I am wondering how do you get the time?"- Sudeep.

"Sudeep, I am blessed and surrounded by the best people and they help me to spare time for all these activities."

"True Nikhil" Sudeep said after taking a long breath "First it's difficult to get such good people, and even if you feel during the selection that they are really good then only time will tell you how good they are?".

"Yes you are correct, Sudeep, lets continue, tell me what would you like to have? *Waise hamre yahan ki pudina chai sab log bahut pasand karte hain* (All our guests like mint tea prepared in our cafeteria)." It was my open offer with no choice.

"Then go for the tea, but no sugar please"- Sudeep.

I asked my office boy to prepare tea, this a great privilege in India that you have people on every front to support you. Otherwise, in the US, it's "help yourself".

"Tell me Sudeep, how I can help you. I got to know you wanted to discuss some challenges of your organization".

"Correct Nikhil, but I want an assurance that our discussion will remain between us. I don't want anyone to know about it, not even my partners."- Sudeep.

It was a bit strange for me, why he wanted to hide from his partners. If this is an organizational problem, then they must know it. I replied "Ya Sudeep we keep all cases confidential here. Any sharing will be done after taking you in confidence whenever required. I already have a background about your company, my team did the profiling so we can directly jump on the challenges."

"Thanks, Nikhil, for understanding. I know you might be thinking about why I am hiding from my partner. So please listen to me, then you will understand. I don't have any wrong intentions."- Sudeep.

"As you know we two friends are running this business, you can say I am the sleeping partner in this business. I have good contacts in the industry so my involvement is limited to bringing strategic accounts and provide guidance whenever required. I am not involved in the day-to-day operations and management, which is being taken care of by my friend, Parag. He is a super talented guy with a versatile personality and has been successfully running the show since its inception. Almost for two years, there are challenges in operations, client retention, marketing, and sales more or less everywhere. A few months back I met one investor in some summit and who had shown interest in our business model. Thereafter, the process got initiated and the investor and his firm evaluated our company from all aspects including our value system, processes, people, clientele, service model, etc. Everything was looking excellent but on the final discussion they raised some concerns and told me that with these concerns they won't be able to move ahead." – Sudeep.

"Okay, and what are their concerns specifically".

"That's the most challenging thing for me to share, they shared concern on my friend's leadership style."- Sudeep.

"Okay, for investors, leadership is a key aspect before making any decision. What are their observations about your friend?"

"Our business model is people-driven, so investors engaged one audit company with our consent. They conducted the survey, interacted with almost 80% of our staff in skip meetings, group meetings, and one-to-one meetings. Based on that they shared the observations. They haven't raised the question on his capabilities and even praise his leadership except for one thing."- Sudeep.

"And what is that one thing?"

"According to them he operates and works with people with biasing, he is surrounded by some sycophant team members. They see it's as one of the core issues. According to them if the captain of the ship is biased then how he can do the justice to the talented people where we are in this business of selling the service of talented people."-Sudeep.

"Hmmm, and what do you think about it, Sudeep? Do you also believe the same thing for Parag?"

"I never saw him from this perspective and I don't judge people and on top of that if they are my colleague cum friend no question about it. I completely trust him and so far he is doing well."-Sudeep.

"Then what's the problem? It could be just one observation by another third-person, so follow your instinct. You should not suspect your friend."

"Yes I agree, and I am not worried that the investor has denied investment in our company. It doesn't matter, but we wanted to grow. And if there is any scope of improvement for Parag or something is wrong in our organization we need to fix it. There could be a possibility which Parag might not be knowing, that his working pattern is making harm to the organization. My intent is not Parag but the organization. And after listening to all these things from an investor I also did my research and it looks like their findings seem to be right. But I am not sure about it. I need your help to investigate the truth."-Sudeep.

"Sudeep, we are not a detective agency or background check company, we consult our clients for business and leadership development."

"Correct Nikhil, I am not asking you to spy on Parag. Just ignore my words, I completely trust him, I want you to help him to improve and bridge the gap. But without letting him know."- Sudeep.

"This is not feasible Sudeep, how I can coach someone who doesn't know that he needs coaching?"

"I understand Nikhil, but Parag will not feel right. He may take this in a completely wrong way, and I don't want to lose my friendship. It's a problem that can be fixed, at the end of the day he is my best friend, and I want to help him without letting him down. Please figure out something. I know you will be able to figure out something."-Sudeep.

"I appreciate your feelings. If business partners keep such understanding then no business may face trouble due to the partner's conflict. But if any time Parag comes to know about this there can be trust issues between both of you."

"No that won't happen as the intention is not to correct Parag. I want to improve my core leadership team including Parag. And everyone has the scope of improvement, there is nothing wrong with it. I want you to work on a leadership program for our company and we will do it with the collaboration of Parag. But I need to customize a program for our organization, I want you to first understand our challenges and based on that propose the program. There could be a possibility that I might be wrong, whatever I said could be just my apprehension based on the investor's inputs. There could be some other challenges, so if you and your team could do the proper research and execute the program, is my expectation."- Sudeep explained his strategy.

I liked the strategy and for me as long as Sudeep can bring all stakeholders on the same page for the program, I don't have any problem. Sudeep agreed on it and my company took that assignment. This program went up to 10-11 weeks, initial 3 weeks in the identification of a problem, and finding the issues and challenges. Thereafter remaining time took into implementation.

But the findings of that company which was planning to invest in Sudeep and Parag's Company was correct. Favoritism was the biggest challenge for Parag, and all other problems were directly or indirectly circling back to it. Interestingly when I presented all the scenario to Parag in one to one meeting and compared with his own and third-person's perspective, he was surprised. It was new learning for him, he said I never saw all these things from this angle, you have opened my eyes, Nikhil.

I made him understand, that leader should not restrict their views, they should keep their eyes open and minds alert to have 360-degree perspective all the time and for all issues, decisions, or appreciation they do. Otherwise knowingly and unknowingly they will be biased, neither it's good for them nor the organization.

The biggest challenge of biased view is either leader loses their best team members or they demoralize them to not perform because with the biased view we don't take the fair decision instead take the biased decision. Favoritism drastically reduces the capacity of listening, which is one of the essential skills for leaders.

Favoritism is 'Natural'

There are people we like and people we are neutral about and some that we don't like at all. It's human nature we feel more comfortable working with people who are aligned with us. It is only natural that we will have an inclination or liking towards some people over others because we are people first and leaders later.

But in a professional environment, we end up working and dealing with all kinds of people. The other thing is while working we develop a relationship with people surrounding us and then it becomes difficult to keep aside the personal and professional sides of relationships. I have seen such a relationship becomes the bottleneck for the leaders, due to this relationship they are unable to make wise decisions or actions and even they lose the authority on such people to suggest or guide anything.

Favoritism leads to Discrimination

As a leader, it is easy to have favorites because there are people more inclined to you, their working style and energies sync far better as compared to others. But over a period these people start taking undue advantage of being favorite. They know that they are on the good books of their leaders, they can 'manage' or I would rather say 'manipulate' the system for their advantages. These people create a hidden wall around their leaders so other people can't reach out to them, and once they succeed in it, favorite people become the proxy leader of the organization. Where they can't be challenged, questioned, or evaluated. Now they have become supreme, even more than the leaders themselves and it becomes their first right on every opportunity, taking credits for other's work, and blaming others for their failures. What else is left except discrimination for others?

On a lighter note, these favorite people are nothing but *'Jamai Raja'* (son-in-law) of the organization. In our Indian culture, the son-in-law is a non-questionable entity. He has the privilege to comment on anything and everything, mock anyone in his in-laws' house, he can even question supreme authority 'father-in-law' and they are still forced to respect him. Besides that, no one dares to speak against him. Similarly, favorite people are like *'Jamai Raja'* (known as *'Jijaji'* too) of the organization and they expect preferential treatment from everyone.

Why leaders have a Favorite?

As I said earlier it's natural to have our favorites, but there is a very thin line to reach in the zone of getting biased due to the favorites and doing injustice to other people. As a leader all people are ours, and being fair with everyone is the primary responsibility of any leader. If a leader feels that some people should not be in their team due to whatever the reasons are, I would say again it's a leadership failure. It's a question of their capability of selecting people to build the right team.

But have you ever thought about why leaders get so dependent on these *'Jijajies'?* These *Jijajies* were born due to the failure or gap in the leadership skill of the leaders. These *Jijaji* are the smart people who identify the gap in their leaders and they volunteer themselves to fulfill that gap, and become the *Jijaji* of the organization. The other reason is when leaders reach in their comfort zone, as they want to enjoy their biggest leadership perk by *'Ji Hazoori'* (Yes Sir), thus *'Jijajies'* get born. It's a sign of weak leadership, the weaker the leader is, the more *Jijajies* will be in the organization. I have some great examples:

- One of the CEOs was not good at English communication and there is no issue with it. Everyone is having their strength and weakness. But the problem occurs when leaders try to cover up the weakness, I do not advocate sharing weakness but if it is visible then there is no point in covering it. That CEO could have an office assistant who can manage this thing, but he was afraid that what people will think of his weakness in English Language? It's a leadership trap that leaders feel that they should be all-rounder.

Very soon one *Jijaji* emerged to help the CEO and started operating his email account, preparing the documents, etc. And Mr. CEO was able to show off his weakness as a strength. But he wanted to keep this secret, and this dependency not only made *'Jijaji'* one of the favorites but also created the opportunity for him to start taking undue advantage.

- The other example is about a leader who was leading the customer account and management team. He was required to maintain a strong relationship with all key customer accounts to dig for more business. But that leader was always having a thought that he has reached this position to enjoy the luxury of bossism, not to go after the clients, doing the calls. In nut-shell he just wanted to avoid his responsibilities but continue to enjoy the position. Many times I heard leaders saying out of frustration 'is this what I am supposed to do?', but they forget to avoid the responsibilities' is different, from 'taking the new responsibilities'.
  Again *Jijaji* came into the picture, he became the proxy of a leader. Started doing all activities which the leader was supposed to do, and as this was the proxy model *Jijaji* leveraged fully by ruling the entire department and taking all undue advantages.

So leader's weakness is, they want to remain leaders but don't want to carry the leadership task. Favoritism takes place in the organization because leaders need such people aka Jijaji to fulfill their desire.

A survey conducted by Georgetown University's McDonough School of Business found that 92% of senior business executives have seen favoritism at play in their promotions processes, including in their own companies. And about 25% of these leaders admitted that they have practiced favoritism themselves.

Favoritism significantly impacts the team member's morale and productivity, causing resentment and a lack of motivation. Any leader needs to have an inclusive team-building culture where every team member feels they are being fairly treated based on their capabilities rather than on their personal relationship with their leaders.

Many people asked me how to spot the sign of a leader promoting favoritism. It is pretty easy, here are few examples:

Office ke Ganesh Ji (Lord Ganesha of the Office)

We all know Lord Ganpati, across all gods he has to be worshipped first in *'Sanatan Dharma'* (Eternal Religion). Many leaders are surrounded by such people as *'Jijajies'* to whom you have to approach 'first' to reach out to the leader. They want other people to worship them, please them to get something done by the leader. And even if someone gets succeed to reach those leaders, again they get redirected to those *Jijajies* for work. This gives Jijaji authority and the first person to reach out to get work done in the organization.

Leader develop Gods

A true leader develops more leaders, but leaders who promote favoritism rather develop Gods. Why god? Strange example? No one can question the god, his decision, blessings, and justice, similarly the leader's favorite people *'Jijajies'* can't be questioned. Whatever they do, it's a blessing to the organization and other people. Even if they did something wrong, the leader takes the frontline and starts to justify what is 'right' in that 'wrong' of those *Jijajies?*

In one of the organization, the CEO had one such *Jijaji*, his key responsibility was no work for him, but to create obstacle in others work, pinpoint other's mistakes, keep complaining, stretching minor things to a larger extent, do whatever is required to show other people in a bad light. And if someone questioned him and tries to show him the mirror, then he makes the hue and cry and turns the table using his influence on the CEO by raising the question of that person's integrity. And to surprise, on many instances, he stopped working for weeks and months, by saying he can't work with such people. CEO used to say in such a situation *"Tu to khali bhi baithtega to bhi value add karega"* (Even if you are sitting idle it still adds value). Now you can imagine when the CEO starts justifying the non-working of *Jijajies,* then what is the motivation for others who are not a part of that favorite gang.

Pehla Haq to Jijaji ka hai (The first claim on anything is reserved for the leader's favorite)

Arjun has a proven track record of finishing all types of assignments, managing difficult and demanding clients, developing a strong relationship with clients, and converting that relationship into bringing more business, positive feedback from the clients. But he was never a choice of his leaders to kick off any new assignment, it was always reserved for Anish (One of the favorites of organization's leaders).

Later if Anish gets bored with the existing assignment or another new exciting assignment comes by or Anish is unable to drive the assignment then leaders used to re-assign to it Arjun or someone else. Even for Anish's incapabilities, others were being blamed.

So this is another sign of favoritism when new projects, assignments are limited to the favorite people despite their capabilities and expertise in managing those.

Sirf Hum-Tum (Only you and me)

It's a pretty obvious sign that someone is favorite if they're accompanying the boss on a business trip to Washington...even though they went along to that conference in San Francisco the month before...and the important meeting in New York the month before that. But aside from missing out on the odd fancy dinner and nice hotel, there's nothing to worry about, right?

When leaders share the learning and exposure opportunities with their team members fairly, it's a commitment to their career growth. But the challenge is when opportunities are limited to their favorites, then others are just listening to their experiences.

In one organization, there were multiple talented people but the default setting for onsite opportunity was limited to *Jijaji* only.

Navratnas (A group of 9 Gems)

King Akbar was an ardent admirer of art and learning. His court was full of many scholars and talented artists. The Nine most learned men in his court were known as Navratnas and Akbar used to take advice from them for important decision makings. Similarly, leaders too have Navratnas (gems) in good and bad ways. We are talking here about the Navratnas who are the product of favoritism.

Asking for input is a sign that a leader respects someone's ideas, observations, and inputs, it's one way of appreciation. People get confident that they are adding value. But you may notice such leaders always seek suggestions, ideas, and inputs from certain people *(Jijajies)* even in an open meeting. They completely ignore others, or if someone makes a valid suggestion, the leader continues to wait until those *Jijajies* don't give their 'Two Cents' advice. The situation becomes worse when leaders go beyond that and they start to seek validation from *Jijajies* even on their ideas, decisions, and actions. In such scenarios, what space is left for others?

Proxy CEO

This is one of the most evident signs that favoritism could be at the workplace. When an employee *(Jijajies)* is subjected to less scrutiny for their performance, or they are never criticized or being ignored for their consistent failures, their leaders protect them by passing the blame of their failure to others. It's almost as if that person is being treated more as a peer than a subordinate. It includes speaking out of place or being allowed to get unsupervised job while everyone else is subject to the third-degree treatment.

In one of the organizations, management had their favorite baby. That baby was allowed to question anyone in the organization irrespective of his knowledge of that domain, he can screw up anyone. Anytime he could blame anyone, use his influence to fire people, play dirty politics, drive parallel agenda, and by chance if he gets stuck in a situation where he is accountable, he starts crying like a baby to get the sympathy of management.

As he was the favorite baby of leaders, he tended to use the cabin of the CEO and sit on his chair whenever the CEO is not around. There is nothing wrong with it, we are living in a flat world. But still, it was giving the wrong message to all employees. May be CEO was open-minded but in general, commitment and accountability are always towards the chair. CEO was in the illusion that he is so open but that baby was smart enough to utilize the power of *Kursi* (posotion). In India, *Sara khel kursi ka hi hai* (Game is all about of position). Many employees started assuming that this baby is so powerful as he was sitting on the CEO's chair so there is no point in confronting him and if that person occupies the chair of their CEO, he can eat up their career too.

These proxy CEO, next to the CEO, the right hand of the CEO, or the left hand of the CEO are not just a threat to the people, they are a threat to the organization and its growth. Because these favorite people don't work for the organization's goal, they work for their personal goals and can go to any extent of manipulation.

Baksheesh (Tip)

Perks are being given when employees perform extraordinarily in their job. But when they start getting perks because they are favorite of their leaders, it's nothing but favoritism. Getting salary on the first day of the month where others are getting on standard day of the month, utilizing a company credit card for a personal expense, accompanying leader on all trips as Stepney (as a spare wheel), getting waived off from all rules and regulation of company are the few examples of perks without the performance and it's known as *Baksheesh* (tip). The other difference is people get perks when they have benefited the organization and *Baksheesh* (tip) when they are pleasing their leaders. This reminds me famous dialogue of the famous Bollywood villain

Amrish Puri *"Mongambo kush hua"*(Boss is happy hence giving the tip).

Sacha Dost (A True Friend)

Sometimes leaders and people develop the relationship outside the office and it's just natural. But issues come when professional and personal territory gets mixed up. And many times leaders have to comprise on the professional front to save the personal relationship. Besides that, these favorites start utilizing their relationship to showcase their closeness to leaders and take undue advantage of others. *"Tumhe maloom hain na mai kiske sath utha baithta hoon*(You know about my network, right?)" that comes in their attitude while talking or communicating with others. This gives the message to others that they are not privileged ones and have to compromise with favorites despite their performance.

Haraphanamaula (All-rounder)

Haraphanamaula is an all-rounder personality, he is the hero of a Hindi movie who can do anything, everything, and anytime starting from romance, fighting with the villain, driving cycle to an airplane, singer, dancer, and many more things. There is nothing that exists in the world which they can't do. Favorites of leaders are also the Hero, can do anything as they are blessed with the superpower of organization.

I was doing one assignment in an IT company and interacted with *Haraphanamaula.* I was wondering do we have such creature in this world who can play any role of solution consultant, solution architect, technical architect, web architect, mobile architect, technical manager, business analyst, functional consultant, cloud technology starting from Azure to Google to Amazon, coding expertise from open source to proprietary technology like Microsoft, front end, database, security, even now I can't recall. Do you think such *Haraphanamaula* can exist without the backing of their leaders?

Besides that, *Haraphanamaula* (all-rounder) can poke his nose anywhere. One day he was recommending to the HR department how to do a screening of candidates, another day he was reviewing the work of the marketing team, very next day was giving training to sales team how to mature the lead, then suddenly he flew to the USA to attend consulting assignment, and suddenly other client faces the issue in software then he was there to fix as a developer and after coming back started working on the organization strategy.

Bus aakhri ek din maine pooch hi liya "Hey prabhu aap kaise itne roop dhar ke ye sari lilaye kar lete hai." Jawab mila, "You know..." (One day finally, I asked that person, "My lord how you can play all the roles", and he responded "You know...")Rest is a mystery.

Any form of favoritism is not good for leaders, this erodes self-confidence in your team members and increases their insecurities. Favoritism is a symptom of poor leadership skills. Essentially, a leader who keeps favorites is not a great leader, regardless of their personal feelings towards a particular person. Good leaders remain thoroughly professional at all times and make decisions based purely on business and performance. When this practice is spurned in favor of personal preferences, it creates an organizational culture and severely negative impact on the effectiveness of the workforce.

As a leader are you trapped in favoritism? Check it out with these question

- Are you giving undue and preferential treatment to some of your team members?
- Are you endorsing and promoting one over the other?
- Are you giving opportunities based on the performance or your personal relationships?
- Are you sharing the information with those people who are not required to be shared?
- Are you constantly overlooking the mistakes and failures of some specific people?
- Are you assigning important tasks and highlighting work done by those preferred ones?
- Are you justifying the failures of your preferred ones to others?
- Are you protecting your preferred from others, if they are made accountable or being questioned for their work?
- Are you offering additional benefits and assistance to your preferred ones which is not available for others?
- Are your preferred people overriding delegation of authority and crippling necessary hierarchy?

"Workplace requires professionalism, not favoritism"
-Jack Welch

7

Aap Ki Adalat

CONFLICT RESOLUTION BY LEADERS

"When leaders resolve the conflict of the team by becoming a judge in making a decision, and act as an advocate to the favorable side, and produce the evidence to prove their judgment"

Some days are special and some days are made special. This was a day made special by the visit of my bestie Ajay aka Ajju. It was always a delight to meet him. He is serving as a navy officer and was visiting the States on some official grounds.

It's been a hectic week so far and just a few minutes with Ajju has taken away all the stress. We were chatting and sipping tea. I had instructed Aashutosh not to disturb me today and to take care of calls and meetings planned for the day.

So all was set and I planned the whole day in my mind. It's a regime from our college days which is called 3B (*Bhai, Booze Aur Bakwas* – Friend, Booze, and Gossip). But as always good things come to an early end. When we were having lunch together Aashutosh came to me and reminded me of a call with Mr. Malhotra.

"Boss I hate to disturb you but it's urgent, you have a call with Mr. Malhotra."

"Oh, I almost forgot about that. Thanks for reminding me Aashutosh". I had scheduled this meeting a long time back and generally, I avoid last-minute cancellation. This practice has set a good example across the board and my team has started to follow that too. And this happened because I knew that the team always imitates the leader and if you want a good culture and practices at your workplace there is a golden rule *"charity begins from home."* If you want your team to be punctual, start being punctual. I have seen many leaders coming to the office at their convenience and managing the timesheets so minutely as some jeweler examining their gems.

"Ajju, I need to take this. I hope you won't mind." I knew he will not. The ultimate luxury with true buddies is that they always understand.

"Please go ahead, work is always a priority." Ajay replied.

"Sure Ajju."

I attended the call. It was from India more, precisely Pune. Mr. Malhotra is CEO of an FMCG company. He has the reputation of a successful businessman and his firm is constantly growing. He has been in this business for decades, and have known the market and his business like the back of his hands. I have done some research on him and found that he is a very acclaimed and renowned businessman. Young entrepreneurs look up to him and seek advice from him. What help does a person of such stature need from my company? I wondered. But Mr. Malhotra wanted to have a call and we have fixed a call for today long ago. I was very curious. That's why I didn't want to miss this call at any cost.

"Hello, Mr.Malhotra."

"Hi Nikhil, How are you."

"I am doing good. Thanks for asking. How are you?"

"I am also good Nikhil, actually not that good, that's why I wanted to have a chat with you."

"Mr. Malhotra, tell me what's bothering you, I'm all ears."

"See Nikhil, I am not sure what the real problem is but I can tell you the issues I am facing right now."

"Please continue."

"To share with you, Nikhil the business is growing and I don't face any challenges there. But in recent times I have been noticing that the drive in the top management is declining which was not the case earlier. The non-productivity among the top managers is becoming noticeable and I have observed often cases of confrontation among themselves."

"Have you identified any reasons for that so far Mr.Malhotra?"

"Not actually, that's the real problem I am facing and that's where I need your help."

"Mr. Malhotra before we proceed further can I ask you some questions."

"Yeah of course."

"Does your organization has a manager playing multiple roles?"

"Yes, a couple of my managers do." Malhotra.

"How do you come to know that there is confrontation among your managers?"

"They have started keeping me in cc in every communication they do among themselves." Malhotra.

"Just because they are keeping you copy in emails you have concluded that they are non-productive." I was a bit surprised by his findings.

"No, that's not the reason. The kind of language they are using in emails makes me worried, either they are justifying how much work they are doing or blaming others for their own success/performance." Malhotra.

"Did you try to stop this or asked why they are doing so?"

"No" Malhotra.

"May I ask why?"

"What harm does it make? Now I know everything that's going around" Malhotra.

"Yet you said it bothers you." Now I was a bit confused about the problem.

"Ummm Yes" Malhotra.

"Have you also noticed non-cooperation among your managers?" Generally, when your team starts justifying or blaming, the first thing they do is not cooperate with each other to create the dependencies. Once dependencies are created people have the opportunity to fail others.

"Yes, Nikhil I have. It was not the case earlier but now I am facing it" Malhotra replied.

"Have you ever had a meeting with such managers whom you think are not cooperating?"

"Ohh for sure I have held a meeting with them."- Malhotra.

"Separately or together?"

"Together."-Malhotra.

"What did you do in that meeting?" I wanted to know the approach of Malhotra.

"I encourage them to bring out all the differences on each other's faces and I listen to both of them." Malhotra proudly replied.

"And then what did you do."

"Then what, in the meeting itself everything was open and in front. They presented their cases and had debates, discussions, and some arguments before making any resolution. I don't think anything else is required." Malhotra said in a judgmental tone, "Ok." I was losing interest.

"Nikhil I am really serious about resolving the conflict, I have sent some of my managers to very expensive soft skills training programs but somehow nothing has worked. That's why I have come to you." Malhotra said in a frustrating tone.

"Mr. Malhotra I understand that you are very serious about resolving the issues and I will try my best to help you out. My team will require to visit your office for a better understanding of the issue. I hope you won't mind." I wanted to finish the call. "Of course not. You are welcome." Malhotra replied.

"And your permission is required to meet and interview some of your employees as well."

"Feel free to do whatever is required from your end." Malhotra.

"Thank you, Mr.Malhotra. Aashutosh will be in your touch in terms of our further engagement and the dates of the visit. Meanwhile, I have taken notes of the things you have told me."

"Thank you, Nikhil. I hope everything will be sorted out. Looking forward to meeting you in person." - Malhotra.

"Be rest assured Mr. Malhotra we will do our best. We will meet soon. Bye Good night"

"Bye Nikhil, good day to you."

I don't know why a smile came on my lips as I hung up the call. I rushed back to the cabin where Ajju was talking over the phone. He knows how to keep himself busy I thought.

"*kya chal raha hai kake* (What's going on)?" I asked Ajju while entering the cabin.

"Nothing much, *Dushyant ko call kiya tha* (I called Dushyant), was telling him about your office. I haven't said it earlier but I am impressed. It's a nice setup you have here, happy to see your progress. Anyways, how was your call?". Ajju.

"It's a usual call of business challenges Ajju, this is what we do day and night."

"Share with me if something is interesting, we are far away from the corporate worlds and their challenges. And somehow I always find it very interesting to read or listen about it." Ajju showed interest to know about the business problem. Someone said that "Grass is greener always on another side", I always find it exciting to listen about the navy and their adventure stories. And my navy friend wants to listen to the corporate stories, amazing. I replied, "Sure happy to share, just take care of not sharing about a client with anyone, client confidentiality mate".

"Ya, ya I agree Nikhil, don't worry about it".

"From what I have understood so far from the brief discussion is that in judicial terms it's an open and shut case of not being able to efficiently manage conflict in an organization."

"Seriously? Is managing conflict a big issue in organizations," Ajju responded in awe.

"Yes, it is. I can understand why you are so surprised. It is because of your armed forces background. It is unthinkable for you to consider conflicts unmanageable. You have unconditional obedience and loyalty across the board but in the corporate, it's a leader's responsibility to have that kind of culture in the organizations. Unfortunately, it is a neglected area and many of the leaders take it for granted and do not invest their time in it. Either they choose to neglect the conflict and wait for them to become a snowball or some choose the easiest path of eliminating the conflict by firing the concerned people. Both are unhealthy for an organization."

"It's interesting, tell me more about it," Ajju said by adjusting himself more comfortably in the chair. It seems he is interested in this.

"See Ajju, workplace conflict is an inevitable phenomenon especially when different employees are put to work together for a common organizational goal."

"You said conflict is inevitable. Is it true?"Ajju.

I replied "Yes. Now try to understand this, what are the major differences employees have. The main difference they may have are -

- Different personalities
- Different backgrounds
- Different ethnics
- Different work styles
- Different perceptions

"Once you have that understanding it will be easy for you to understand why I said workplace conflict is inevitable."

"That's true, they have these differences," Ajju responded with a nod. "Now I understand that workplace conflict is inevitable, do the organizations have some conflict management systems in place."

"Very rightly observed, Ajju, conceptually it seems they should have one but on the contrary, most of the mid-size organizations don't have them."

"But why? Do they not care for their people?"Ajju sounded irritated.

"Easy Ajju, don't get so impatient. Let me explain it to you. Every leader of an organization have their reasons, most of them are very common"

- Firstly leaders fail to understand the cost of conflict an organization has to bear. They think it's a natural phenomenon that arises and fades away in its own due time. There is no need to pay too much attention to it.
- Secondly, most of the leaders misunderstood conflict resolution with grievance handling. They put both in one basket and treat them the same. Once they have grievance handling mechanisms in their organization they consider their job is done.
- Thirdly, leaders think that they can handle conflicts among teams or in their organization easily when they arise. So there is no need for such a system.
- Fourthly some leaders think that they have made a perfect organization and it will not happen in their organization. It's for others.
- Moreover, for some leaders there is only one way to handle conflict resolution is to fire the concerned employees immediately. It is like chopping off the infected organ rather than curing it. This approach has some serious implications.

- And finally, the last and most interesting one, few leaders wait for conflicts to happen in the organization.

"Leaders wait for conflict to happen, are you kidding?"Ajju's surprise gave me giggles.

"Yes, Ajju it's true. Some leaders wait for conflict to happen so that they will have the opportunity to showcase their coaching abilities to the organization. This is the time for them to distribute their *'Gyan ka Gulkand'* (It's a sarcastic Hindi Idiom which means when someone tries to enforce their knowledge) to their employees. They literally die for it and see conflict among employees as an opportunity for satisfying their mentoring and coaching desires."

"You can't be serious" Ajju was serious and for him, it was difficult to digest this fact.

"Ajju, I am serious. I have witnessed such leaders who don't even care how much damage it causes to the organization but they prefer to satisfy their hunger of being a coach and mentor no matter how pathetic they are in that."

"For you to share the example of today's call the CEO can sense that there is a conflict arising among his top managers as they have started copying him in all of their internal communication which is not desired at all. The CEO must take immediate steps to such practice and intervene but on the contrary, he is allowing it, even after knowing that it will lay down a foundation of such practice across the organization and will harm the overall culture of the organization and harmony among employees."

"Then why does he do that."Ajju was puzzled

"There can't be any specific reason for that he might be doing it may because he wants to know what's going around on the manager's level or maybe wants to make all the managers insecure in their own positions to strengthen his leadership position as the elder of the house to whom all the cry baby go."

"So he didn't do anything at all" Ajju asked again.

"Of Course he did. He called the meeting of the two managers having a conflict."

"That makes sense," Ajju said.

"It looks that way. Calling a face-to-face meeting is indeed a good start but the important thing is what you do in such a meeting as a leader.

This CEO for an instance in the meeting encourages the employees to bring all the issues to the table. He gives them the confidence of a safe environment in which they can pour out their heart, encourages them to speak freely. Now so far it is good. When they start sharing their problems ending up putting the blames of noncooperation, distrust, etc. on each other. He as a leader only listens and takes no action."

"Now, this has some severe consequences like firstly this leaves both the employees disappointed because they were in hope of some conclusion brought to the issue but none was delivered. This impacts their trust in the leader and his leadership. If the decision of the leader comes in anyone's favor it must disappoint the other but no decision or no conclusion impact both of them greatly. Secondly, the things which are not open or they haven't said to each other, now they have done that and worse, in front of the CEO. This will remove all checks from them and from now onwards there is a huge possibility that they will be more vocal against each other and cause serious damage to the culture and environment of the organization."

"Aise leader lagaate hai aap ki adalat, jisme ilzam khud lagaate hai jawab khud dete hai par it is never meant to reach any conclusion. Haan entertainment poora hota hai and you know no one realizes that the soul purpose of aap ki adalat is entertainment for a leader." (Such leaders make a dramatic environment by creating a courtroom situation where two parties are blaming each other and they enjoy the conversation by becoming a judge. The purpose is not to resolve the conflict but to showcase and enforce their knowledge with some judgment. The biggest problem with judgment is that one of the parties is going to be dissatisfied.)

"Ohh I see, but If I may ask what actually causes the conflict in any organization," Ajju asked with a curious face.

"Interesting question, as we have discussed earlier that people come into an organization with different backgrounds and they are assigned different roles in different departments. It is very natural to have a difference in opinion about how work should be done in the company based on their beliefs of each other's functional roles. And still, there are some other common reasons which cause conflict in any organization, they are,"

- Task Interdependencies - The greater the extent of task interdependence among employees or teams the greater are the chances of conflict if the goals and expectations are different.
- Lack of Resources-When employees and teams have to share

common resources and these resources are scarce then the conflict can become quite unavoidable.

- Role ambiguity: When the role and responsibilities are not well defined, then the person who is carrying out these responsibilities will not perform as per the expectation of others, thus causing a conflict. because his role is not clearly defined.
- Jurisdictional Ambiguities: When the jurisdiction of the employee or department is not clearly defined they end up encroaching on each other's areas unknowingly, therefore causing a conflict.
- Communication Breakdown: The absence of a well-defined communication process can cause conflict. When communication is misunderstood or when information is withheld, conflict arises.

"It sounds right and seems that a conflict can arise anytime anywhere."Ajju was listening and nodding, then he asked "what a leader should do to resolve a conflict?"

"Conflicts are the avenues where true leadership comes into play. Remember the times when we used to play in the university cricket team. Dushyant was our captain and there was always a quarrel on every petty issue. Two batsmen arguing over opening the innings, bowlers arguing to bowl with the new ball as it swings more and gives an extra edge to the bowler, or having an argument to field in the slip as it requires less running. Conflicts were everywhere and before every match but it was Dushyant who intervene at right time and resolved them. The roles were clearly defined and communicated, the goal was clearly placed and we ended in winning the tournament."

"Ya I remember, those were the days but I have never looked at this way of a leader resolving the conflict. Dushyant never seemed to control anything he was there just as a friend." Ajju was staring at the wall like he was trying to recall.

"That's the quality of a leader Ajju. He never seems to impose the leadership but it is always there".

"Han yaar sahi hai, ab sochta hu to sab clear aur simple lag raha hai. Never realized at that time (You are right, now I am realizing how Dushant was leading and it looks simple and straightforward)" Ajju was smiling.

- "Now coming to your question about how to resolve a conflict in an organization. But first, let me tell you what a leader must not do when a conflict arises".
- No action is a disaster, every leader should avoid falling into a trap

of doing nothing or ignoring the problem.
- Labeling the employees as problem creators or crybaby or complainer.
- Not giving importance to secrecy and making the conflict public.
- Throw the employees in a loop of long processes

"These are the things that will worsen the situation and will have more severe implications in the organization."

"Interesting but then what a leader should do?"Ajju said I can sense the rising curiosity.

"Now what a leader should do can be summarized in following actions, firstly whenever a conflict arises he should make sure employees are clear about organizational goals and priorities and reinstate the importance of goals against relationships".

- Consider taking leverage of conflicts as an opportunity for team building.
- Should define acceptable behavior and should broadcast that across the floor.
- Plan towards a win-win outcome and strictly avoid win-lose or lose-lose scenarios.
- Listen to everyone involved and hear their views, intervene with an open mind.
- Should do a root cause analysis to reach the core of the issue which will help to avoid any further conflict in the organization.

"How a leader can do that is a different conversation altogether but that might need a whole night and I am already hungry."

"Ah, I almost didn't notice it's dark already. My mind got the good food, and now my stomach is giving an alarm", Ajju replied.

"Ya mate let's go we have a lot to catch up."

"Let's go then," Ajju said while wearing his jacket.

• • • • • •

Check out the following questions about how are you resolving the conflicts.

- Have you noticed a decline in the productivity of your team due to conflicts?
- Have you lost some good people from your organization due to conflicts not being handled properly?
- Have you neglected the conflicts among your teammates because you didn't know how to address that?
- Do you have a conflict resolution mechanism in your organization?
- If yes, is your team aware of it?
- Do conflicts end up in grievances of the teammates?
- Do you wish to have conflicts be addressed constructively?

"Peace is not the absence of conflict, it is the ability to handle conflict by peaceful means."

-Ronald Regan

8

Beta Tumse Na Ho Payega

DEDICATION vs DELEGATION IN LEADERSHIP

"When a leader starts believing that people can't do their work perfectly unless he/she intervenes"

It's a Saturday morning, and the most important ritual is to have a long call with mom in India. My discussion is not just limited to family matters, we discuss a lot about what is happening in our surroundings, experiences in our day-to-day life. Many times I get so much insight with her wisdom and rich experience that, it not only helps me with effective parenting but dealing with people-related issues at the workplace.

"Good morning, Dad"- Just heard the voice of my elder daughter Jiya.

"Good morning dear, so early *bacha* it's a weekend". (We use *bacha* in Hindi to address kids out of love.)

"I know Dad, but there is a lot of work to finish today."-Jiya said. I could see from her face how tough it was for her to wake up early on Saturday. I continued, "So your internship is finishing next week?"

"Dad, you are so engrossed with your schedule that you forget my training was over yesterday. This is not fair"- Jiya in complaining mode.

"Oops, sorry I missed it. Anyways how was your first exposure with the corporate world."

"It was good, I got to know how this world is completely different from what we learn in books. So overall good experience and exposure. But I came across various cases during my short tenure in that company and that made me confused about certain fundamentals I have learnt. Not able to decide what is right or wrong?"- Jiya said in an astonished voice.

"What happened, something went wrong with you?"

"All good, Dad just confused with some of the things which I am experiencing in office. Not able to get an understanding of what is right or wrong. From my perspective, it looks fine, but when colleagues discuss it looks wrong."-Jiya with a confused face.

"Aha, now I got it what is bothering my *bacha.* That's called exposure to the outer world. Now you have an understanding of why an internship is important. It's like a grand rehearsal before anyone starts their professional journey".

"Dad, I need your time today as I have to compile a report and submit it to my college next week. I hope you don't have any plans for today."-Jiya.

"No other plans, full day is for you my sweetheart. Let's get ready and meet at breakfast then we can discuss the rest of the day".

My daughter Jiya is doing a Bachelor's in Management with a specialization in people management. Time flies, I didn't realize when my little Jiya grew up and started moving into corporate life. Only one year is left for her to finish the course, they have a 4-month internship to be done at the end of the third year. Earlier I thought that she can do it from my company but later on, dropped the idea that due to me she may not have the true experience. So she joined a three years old start-up which she got from the college placement cell for her training.

• • • • • •

"Whats in breakfast?"- Jiya asked Avaantika.

"Today we have Jiya's favorite *Podi Masala Idli with sambhar* (A south Indian dish)"-Avantika.

Before anyone else gives the feedback on breakfast my younger one Ami got upset, she likes sandwich and conveys her displeasure. Avantika smartly negotiated that lunch will be her choice with *Chola-bhatura* (A north Indian dish) and looks like Ami got settled very quickly on her *didi's* (In Hindi elder sister is called as *Didi*) choice.

"So let's start Jiya, I am really excited to listen to your experiences. All your learning will be the stepping stone for your career".

"Sure Dad and some of the things are not part of my internship scope but shared by other colleagues over there so I am curious to understand those as well."- Jiya.

She continued, "Although they are a sound startup but ventured in many lines of business like product development, services, consulting, looks like whatever new and exciting comes in the market they try to grab it. Which is really cool, I got a chance to touch upon many business areas."

"The most exciting thing that happened to me was that I got an opportunity to work with the organization's COO. Still, it's difficult to believe that one of the topmost people of the organization is interacting with the trainee. Isn't cool?"-Jiya with full of excitement.

"Ya, that's true Jiya."

"Even he said that he will help in reviewing my project submission to the college. I admire him, he is a role model for me. But no one in the office likes him, everyone is trying to just avoid him."- Jiya's pursed lips were showing that she was not happy with her colleagues.

"Hmm, okay there could be some reason."

"Dad don't smirk at me, I have great respect for the COO."- Jiya.

"No-no Jiya I am not smirking at you, I am just trying to gulp what you are saying. If you believe COO is good then he is good. Why you are confused?"

"Dad I trust my colleagues. They are also good and talented people, so if they are saying something then there has to be a reason and my confusion is coming from there. When I am with the COO, he looks correct but my view changes as soon as I listen to my colleagues."- Jiya said.

"Jiya I am trying to understand, so there is a leader who is the COO of the organization and his team, your colleagues and it looks like the team doesn't like him, correct?"

"Yes, dad you are right. I want to understand where the gap is, is it a leader's issue or it's a problematic team itself. You know organization leadership is one of my core areas of research for this internship and understanding this would help me to make my assignment better. "-

Jiya finally opens her card, that's what the objective is.

"Jiya can you share some of the scenarios or instances which you have observed, experienced, or if someone has shared. It will help me to understand the context."

"Sure dad, let me start with COO, he is a very helpful person, running day-in-day-out on the floor to help everyone. He works with everyone and assisting them to finish their task. Every morning he is running behind people to get the work done. He is always eager to provide the inputs whether its technical department, operations, recruitment, project management even on a personal level." – Jiya was speaking flawlessly and I can sense she is very impressed with her COO.

"Dad, one of my colleagues Barbara was working with the recruitment department and was leading a small team there. She is a seasoned recruitment professional with a vast experience of 12 years in the industry. She was my first point of contact in the company and did all formalities on my joining. She is responsible for overseeing the sourcing, interviewing, and hiring of new employees. She has become my good friend and there is a lot to learn from her about relationships and network building. Due to her profile, she is closely working with the COO. But I observed her that every meeting with the COO ends up with the frustration and its keep piling up."- Jiya.

"Have you ever discussed with her what is the issue, why she is frustrated with the COO", my curiosity was increasing?

"According to Barabra, COO is always ready with his '2 cent' advice whether she is looking for it or not. If she prepares the job description for the new recruitment requirement, either COO rewrites it or redefines the whole description. Every time she has to stand behind him when he is rewriting the documents prepared by her as he wanted to guide her. If there is less inflow of candidates for interview then the COO teaches her how to search the candidates on the indeed job portal. In a nutshell, whatever Barbara does COO has to say something or other things."- Jiya.

"Then Barbara could be an underperformer and less efficient, maybe not meeting the expectation of your COO".

"I don't think that's the case. As she doesn't have these issues with the CEO, she is working with all C-level executives in the company and everyone is praising her work. Last month she got an award for showing great performance and quality of work. The only challenge is with the COO. He doesn't leave any opportunity to train her, whereas she doesn't require the training in her key skill area. That's her domain, Barbara always says review my work, give me the feedback I am ready to improve and rectify. But don't teach me how to do my task. Or at least wait until I finish then give me 2-cents advice. But please don't poke the nose every time."

"One day there was some payment term issue with a vendor who was doing staffing for the company. Barbara missed to inform the vendor about the latest revised payment terms and vendor raised the concerns over it. COO immediately jumped in it as a savior. First, he scolded her for a very minor issue, although she was confident that her reputation is very good with the vendor and she will be able to manage the situation without any impact. And the same thing happened, Barbara was able to manage the issue with just a single meeting with the vendor, everything was settled. COO hardly contributed anything during the meeting, but later he projected across the company that there was a big issue due to Barbara's mismanagement and he had to jump in to fix it. When she got to know, it was very demoralizing for her." – Jiya.

"Dad, why the COO is doing all these things? On one part, he is micromanaging and on another part trying to steal the credit by making her image wrong."- Jiya.

"Jiya, some leader think *agar vo chai banaane me haath nahin lagaenge to chai meethi nahin hogee, par unko maloom nahi hai chai shakkar daalane se meethi hotee hai, na ki unke haath lagaane se* (Some people feel if they don't give any guidance in making tea/coffee it won't be sweet. But they forget tea/coffee becomes sweet by adding sugar, not with the guidance). There are two things often mixed by the leaders, hand-holding and delegation. Hand-holding is aimed at improving the employee's performance or help them attain a required level of knowledge or skill. Whereas, delegation is aimed at reducing their workload so they can focus on important tasks and allow the subordinates to grow in the process."

"If a leader delegates a task to a subordinate, the subordinate is expected to complete the task on their own. The leader shouldn't get involved unless required. By micromanaging, you are essentially defeating the purpose of delegating. The key point here is to trust the employee to perform the task on their own. They may require some guidance in the beginning, but don't be an overbearing presence."

"The other mistake which a leader does in a delegation of work, they allocate the task, rather than the goal to their teammates. That doesn't give them clarity on what needs to be achieved and there will always be a gap in expectation and execution. The goal is nothing but the outcome which the leader has in his/her mind, but that cannot be translated through the task. If you are giving just the task then you can't expect the outcome as people will just finish the task. This makes either the leader frustrated or makes him a micromanager, constantly reviewing the work. At the same time, it increases the frustration of people as well, because of the absence of purpose they don't' feel accomplishment and unless they don't achieve what their leaders are expecting, they end up doing task after task. This is a case with your COO, either he is not clear or making his team clear about his expectation. Which makes him constantly poke his nose in other's works by frequently giving them advice."

"But Dad it's an ultimately more loss for a leader, why they do so? " – Jiya.

There is no single reason for it, in reality, their apprehensions force them to do it. Let me give you some more interesting insight.

Atra Tatra Cha Sarvatra (Here, there and everywhere I exist)

Many leaders constantly need acknowledgment from their team members, they feel if they don't get involved in everything, that may create a problem for their existence. So they create opportunities to get involved in everything in the name of 'active involvement' and expect their team is getting validation from them in whatever they do. Leaders feel that doing this makes their leadership more relevant. Moreover, this pleases the leader that people are reaching out to them, frankly speaking for many that is the main goal to reach in a leadership position.

Everyone wants to be liked, but there's a line between being the strong leader that everyone admires and being a people pleaser. It takes a lot of effort, time, and dedication that people start admiring you. Hence, the easiest way for that to happen is to force people to please leaders. Such leaders don't empower their team members which increases their dependency on the leadership and people are forced to reach out to them every time they do anything. That helps them to create an artificial aura and feeling of *'Atra Tatra Cha Sarvatra'* (Here, there and everywhere I exist) by existing everywhere.

"I am getting the clarity Dad, but there will always be some dependencies on leaders. We can't do and should not do everything on our own. We always look upon our leaders for decision making."- Jiya.

"That's right Jiya, people are always looking towards their leaders. But what I am saying is that leaders should get involved where they are required not everywhere and every time. If they are, it's a weak sign of leadership. A leader should get involved when they are needed, if they are engaged in everything they won't be able to do their leadership work."

"Hmmm, Dad, I am recalling one incident Barabara has shared with me. She is responsible for organizing happy hours every Friday, after 2 PM we had a dance party followed by snacks and beer. Barabara's frustration is that every time she has to prepare the estimate including menu item, vendor details, etc, and get it approved by the COO. She says approval is not just limited to cost estimates, COO has always commented on the selection of menu and vendor. But I am unable to understand why she is so concerned if the COO is reviewing something and giving his input. She should not be frustrated." – Jiya.

"No *beta* (it is used to address son/daughter in the Hindi language) that's not the case. COO doesn't need to get involved whenever the party is to be organized. It's a regular event. Your COO has to just set the expectation and if things are getting deviated then he should be involved. For example, he can set the budget, so every time there is no need to get his approval on estimates. He can only be approached if an additional budget is required. He can also set up the rules for selecting the menu and vendor, which will not only make Barabar's life easy but also save his time which he spent every week. This is the way leader should empower their team members to make a decision, if by any chances things go wrong then they should be able to guide them. Otherwise, if they are getting involved every time, then what is the purpose of their leadership?"

"Yes, Dad leaders have to create the toll gates to review and monitor the work of their team members and allow their people to drive on the career highway. This will make sure that people are getting freedom and flexibility to do their work and at the same time leaders are also ensuring by putting check and balances that they are being aligned with the vision. No one gets distracted, it may be a win-win situation."- Jiya.

"Well said Jiya, the biggest problem is people don't realize that leadership is a skill. It doesn't come with age and experience. As we learn all other skills, in the same way, one has to groom this skill too and it is not easy to learn and practice. The organization may give you the title, make you the boss or manager but leadership has to be earned.

Until people don't accept you, you won't be a leader. Unfortunately, in industry leadership profiles are being given based on the length of years one spent in their career."

"It's called experience dad."- Jiya.

"Ya, you can say but I see from a different perspective. It's someone's job tenure, we cannot say just an experience. Experience is how mature you are in dealing with people and situations, it all depends on how much you have learned and implemented. With the same qualification and the same number of years in the job, two people cannot have the same experience."

"It's cool dad, I understand what you are trying to say about the experience."- Jiya.

"Yes Jiya and when someone becomes a leader but doesn't know about the leadership, they get into the trap of becoming the hero."

"Hero??? Like Rajnikant and my favorite Robert Downey Jr." – Jiya was surprised to know that leaders can be a hero.

"Yes because heroism is the easiest shortcut of society to become acceptable to everyone. Such leaders desperately look for the crisis or create a situation by interfering here and there and put themselves into the situation regardless of whether they are required or not for resolving the issue. Initially, it works, the crisis is averted and the leaders look like a hero. But the long-term impact of such actions can be devastating to the individual, the team, and the organization."

"But what's wrong in it, It's good to have such a leader who is always willing to save the team?"- Jiya.

No beta, it's a trap and never-ending cycle of heroism. The leader sees a crisis and jumps in to save. The people see that their leader is going to handle all of the issues and thus, back off when they occur. The leader sees that the team is neither willing nor capable to handle challenges, which serves to reinforce the need for heroism. And the cycle begins again, with each occurrence serving to solidify the pattern of heroism.

These leaders (Heroes) do not apologize for their mistakes and the negative impacts of their behavior on others, as they feel that their hero status justifies their behavior. The leader acts like a steamroller with a single focus, saying things like, "This was an emergency situation. I can't worry about people's feelings."

Heroic Leaders exhibit several key behaviors. First, for the Heroic Leader, information is power. They need to know everything that is happening and tend to act as though they are aware. They need to have all of the information and manage others by knowing more than they do. This leads to micromanagement, as by micromanaging the things they can be on top of the information.

Ek myaan mein do Talavaaren nahin rah sakatee (There cannot be two swords in one scabbard)

Heroic leaders are always hesitant to share or are delegating the works to their team members because they fear if their teammates do more effectively. their value will be decreased. So they make sure either they do it on their own or keep their people in dark by allocating the work in bits & pieces so later on they can assemble the things and present it as they have done it. Such leaders perceive a threat that their superiors might replace them with brighter and better subordinates if independent work is allocated to them. Like your COO, he never tells you the purpose why he wants some work to be done, he will give you only the task so he can get the raw work done from you and then shape it according to the purpose. As you never know the purpose of the work, you will not be able to relate even if it comes in front of you. When you don't know, you won't be able to claim your credit.

The other reason is some heroic leaders start comparing themselves with their teammates but they forget they will no more be evaluated based on their efforts, instead, they will be assessed based on their team performance.

I am Supreme

Heroic leaders always need to be right and believe that they are the only ones who really know how to do the task well. These leaders have a fear of failure and care more about getting things done right than they do about empowering their people. This desire for correctness minimizes delegation and stifles creativity and risk-taking. They see the task as a key part of their authority or status. It gives an ego kick out of being the Supreme; doing things themselves makes them feel important, powerful, and in control. They worry that delegating work to someone else means they will not be able to assert their authority.

The Supreme feeling in leaders starts from the opinions that their team is useless and doesn't know anything, then they start to treat them that way. Eventually, team members fail and the leader's belief comes true. Then heroic leader gets the opportunity to say "I told you so", to anybody who will listen. I was right – they weren't good enough to do the job.

Meri Marzi (Whatever I wish or I think)

Heroic leaders fail to delegate because they lack confidence in their own understanding of the road ahead, and they don't want to embarrass themselves. Others simply find it hard to communicate the whys and the hows, or they are easily frustrated by team members who are struggling. The focus of these leaders is stuck in micromanaging and they fail to visualize the bigger picture thereby unable to set clear expectations while delegating work. This leaves team members confused and frustrated at work.

During one of my assignments, I came across a very interesting incident. The Operation Head reached out to the CEO of the company for some financial approval. CEO asked the operation head, "What is your position in the company?"

He replied, "I am the Operation Head of the organization."

"Then do you think my operation head needs to approach me for such small approval, you are free to take your decisions and let me work on other areas?" CEO replied by showing displeasure that despite his empowerment people are reaching out to him.

That makes the Operation Head very happy and empowered. After some time he approved the loan of 50K to one of the employees. As it was in his limit to approve based on the last discussion he had with the CEO. But to his surprise, one day CEO called him, "Have you approved the loan?"

Operation Head said, "Yes sir". CEO with lost face responded, *"Yaar pooch to lete* (You could have asked me)". That makes the operation head confused when he approached him for approval *"to poocha kyon?* (why you have asked)" and when he approved the loan, CEO said *"pooch to lete* (Could have asked)". Operation head was like *"chahte kya ho* (What do you want Mr. CEO)."

As heroic leaders are not clear about their purpose of work, they keep changing their expectations, and whatever the result comes, good or bad they change their words accordingly.

Aaj to mai bhaut Busy hoon (Today I am completely occupied)

Heroic leaders act like they are too busy and make the people around them feel unimportant and unheard. It's a common excuse of the heroic leaders not delegating work because they don't have that much time to explain everything to someone else. They consider it a waste of time as it requires more effort and instead of answering other person's questions they should finish the task.

Heroic leaders want to invest time in establishing themselves as a hero rather than grooming others, they make assumptions like "she wouldn't want to do this" or "he's not good enough for that". They refuse to have a conversation with their team to understand their challenges in getting work done. Instead, they expect their team members to come forward and tell them this information. Unfortunately, not all people are comfortable with their leaders, so this may never happen! Heroic leaders expect their team to step up instead of asking them. However, everybody is different. An introvert teammate may be great for their next opportunity. But the chances are, they won't run-up to their leaders and shout that in their face. It's up to leaders to offer opportunity, rather than simply expecting the most confident people to grab it.

"Ya dad, true leadership is about how you are aligning your teammates with the common goal and working towards it by sharing work and responsibilities along with empowering them. It's not how leaders do as an individual, it's how their team can achieve. It's a great conversation, now I have enough learning to make my report. Sometimes I will bring Barbara here, she will be happy to learn how she can deal with this situation."-Jiya

"Ya sure, anytime".

• • • • • •

Are you also in the trap of becoming a heroic leader? Check out these questions.

- Do you believe that you can do the work better than others most of the time?
- Do you believe it's better to finish the work on your own rather than getting done by the others?
- Do you always have apprehension that others will mess up the work?
- Do you believe that if I'm not doing the actual work, what value am I adding?
- Do you feel that your team is not capable enough to finish their work without your help?
- Do you feel afraid that someone else might do the work more effectively?
- Do you find it hard to like people who are not taking your

endorsement of their work and doing independently?

- Are you afraid of taking more smart and capable people into your team?
- Do you see questions from the team members as obstacles in your work?
- Do you need acknowledgment from people when you are helping them?

"A leader is someone who can do everything himself. But let other people help him."

-Don Littner

9

Mera Vachan Hi Hai Mera Shasan

MY COMPANY, MY RULE

"When leaders make all the choices or decisions based on their own beliefs and do not involve anyone"

Kem cho Nikhil Bhai (How are you Nikhil). I looked back, it's Jignesh. *"Maja mama Jignesh bhai* (I am good Jignesh)", I replied, In the Hindi language Bhai is a brother and in Gujarat state of India people add Bhai after the name out of respect.

"Su vaat che, tame gujarati sekhi lidu (That's great have you learned the Gujarati Language)?"- Jignesh with full of surprise.

I quickly replied before he added anything, *"Jignesh bhai bus itni hi aati hai, isse aage aap kuch bolenge to samaj nahi aayega* (Jignesh I learned a bit now, if you will continue to speak in Gujarati I may not understand)".

"Are koi chinta ki baat nahi, isse aage hum aap ko sikha denge (No worries I will help you in learning). Good to see you here." -Jignesh.

Jignesh is the President of "Bay Area Desi Professional Network & Outreach". It's a forum of Indian professionals working on the leading profiles in and around of San Francisco bay area. Most of the members are either leading startups or mid-sized organizations as a C-Level executive or as a founder/co-founder. This forum mainly conducts training sessions, workshops by inviting various industry experts and leaders to share their experiences, challenges and how do they overcome those, so their members can get benefit from them.

I got associated with this forum two years back with their expert panel. Jignesh was working with a company which we consulted and from there, our friendship started. He is one of the most enthusiastic people I have ever met. Sometimes I think about how he gets time for all these activities from his busy schedule, he is also associated with various Gujarati and Indian forums.

Today I came here to participate in an open forum for leadership challenges. I liked the format, it doesn't have the typical structure of a forum with one-way communication where speakers are just addressing the participants. Instead, participants share their challenges and experts share their opinion to start the discussion where other participants can also contribute.

"Who else is invited to the expert panel," I asked Jignesh while walking towards the auditorium.

"Are apne Sodi Saheb, CFO consulting wale (Mr.Sodi from the CFO consulting is part of the expert panel.)." Jignesh quickly replied. "He is already here and having breakfast. The program will start after 15 minutes, by that time you can enjoy breakfast. I have arranged Gujratri specialty *fafda-jalbi* (a famous Gujarati dish)."

"No Jignesh Bhai, I already had breakfast."

"Nikhil bhai, aap chinta na kare, pura desi menu hai (Don't worry Nikhil we have Indian menu). We have arranged your favorite *Samosa* (An Indian Snack) also." – Jignesh.

That's another quality of Jignesh, his hospitality. He makes sure to bring simile on everyone's face. He knows very well that *Samosa* is my favorite. *"Jignesh Bhai ab to nashta karna hi padega* (Now I have to take the breakfast after knowing the delicious menu)". While doing our chit-chat, we reached the breakfast area.

"Good morning Sodi, *ki haal chal* (How are you?)", I waved at Sodi.

Vikas Sodi is from Delhi, after completing his CA from India he came to the states 15-16 years back. Then did his CPA from here. After working with multiple organizations he started his own consulting firm 5 years back. His company is providing part-time CFO mainly to startups. We got connected 3 years back while working for the same client. Post that, in many places I have recommended his services and he did the same thing for me. It's a mutual understanding, but our goal is to serve the customer.

"I am good Nikhil, What's up. Sorry I started the breakfast, was feeling hungry."- Sodi replied.

"That's fine Sodi, I already had breakfast but you know Jignesh Bhai when he insists you can't say no."

"Ye lijye aap ki plate (please take your plate)." Jignesh offered me a plate.

"Are Jignesh bhai aap kyo kar rahe hain (Why you are doing this formality Jignesh Bhai), I will take it."

"Nikhil bhai bhale hi hum US main hai par hain to Indian. Host hone ka kuch to dharm karne dijiye (Although we are living in USA Nikhil we are still Indian and being a great host is our part of the culture)". Jignesh.

"So how is the business Sodi". I asked. "It's going great, the more startups in the bay area, the more business I will have."- Sodi.

"That's true Sodi and most of the startups need the services you provide. Because most of the startups are driven by technocrats or subject matter experts. They do have amazing business models but that doesn't work because of poor financial decision-making." I added my views.

"True it's a challenge a lot of the time, startups try to do everything on their own, and tend to be built by visionaries and creative types, but they don't really understand the importance of the financial side of things."- Jignesh said.

"Yes and that's where we pitch in, but the problem is many people don't know the value of having the CFO in place. People compare them with the accountants, but they forget that the accountant is just for bookkeeping and CFO is to strategize the financial planning of the organization. But I am seeing a significant change in the mindset now, so it's good for us." – Sodi replied to both of us.

"We are left with the 5 minutes to start the program, let's go," I said.

"Ya sure, let's go"- Jignesh nodded his head.

We reached the auditorium hall, there were almost 45-50 participants from all age groups. Seating arrangements were made formal, so it doesn't look like training or seminar. I always prefer discussion-based training where everyone is participating rather than one-way communication where one person is constantly speaking and others are just listening *(I believe so)*.

"Everyone please take your seats, we have our expert panel here, so we are about to start."- Jignesh announced.

In the next 5 minutes, everyone gets settled, Jignesh introduced me and Sodi. He had set up the agenda and format of the program. "In the next two hours, we will be discussing the real-time challenges of leadership. These challenges are either faced by you, as a leader, or facing from leadership. We have our expert panel here Nikhil Chaudhary and Vikas Sodi, they will help you to address those challenges but it's not just limited to the experts. All members present in this room are having a great experience and are in the leading position, so they can also suggest the solution. Overall we want that everyone is engaged. One person will start sharing the challenge and this will initiate the discussion, I will moderate the session and will try not to exceed more than 10 minutes for one problem. Do you have any other questions?"

Looks like everyone was good to start, "Just wanted to add one disclaimer, during the discussion on leadership challenges you may feel that discussion is pointing towards you. But that's up to you, how you take it, be neutral, see your leadership challenges as a third person. Then if you have any takeaways from the discussion to improve your leadership, implement it otherwise you can just leave it." I added because many times I see people feel offended during the discussion and such a good session gets diverted where people start to justify themselves and blaming others.

"So who is the opener of today's session?"- Jignesh Bhai asked the audience. There was a great silence, I have always experienced whether it's an office meeting or an open ses sion, whoever is the first one to start always has a good question. Everyone thinks lets somebody ask then I will, *"Pehle app pehle app ke chakkar mai kafi time kharab ho jata hai* (Time gets wasted when everyone thinks that someone else will start)."

"Let me start", I saw one mid-age person said. "My name is Kamal, and I am the co-founder of my company and we are working in the Caregiver Sector."

"That's great, let's have a round of applause for Kamal to kick off this session. Yes, Kamal what challenges do you have?" Sodi asked, looks like he was happy that without wasting much time session got started. Otherwise always experts have to start.

"I proudly say that I am a leader who believes in the 'open door' policy, I am ready and willing to hear out my employee's complaints, challenges, and take action to rectify whatever situation which have came up. I am so transparent that I have designed my office cabin with plain glasses so everyone can see what their leader is doing. However, in the majority of instances when teammates face any challenges they prefer not to come up, despite having an open-door policy and such a transparent environment. I fail to understand what else people expect from their leader." – While speaking Kamal prided himself on being an "open door" flag bearer and at the same time, he was frustrated as well.

"Thanks, Kamal, we have a great case to start our discussion today. Is anyone else who faced a similar problem" – Jignesh asked the audience. Many people gave their affirmation, so it looked like a common problem.

"Just wanted to repeat my disclaimer that it requires courage to share these challenges, our goal is to look into the problem not to judge the person. I request everyone to follow the gist of this session to make it fruitful." Once again shared my thought, as I was very apprehensive that discussion should not become in to a war zone.

"Now let's discuss the challenge as shared by the Kamal, anyone wants to contribute," I asked the audience but looks like no one is keen to touch such a sensitive topic.

"Kamal, in my view having proud of your personal preference of being an open door is the first challenge."

"But Nikhil it's a policy, not my preference, why we can't have proud in some good policies of an organization." Kamal immediately jumped as soon as I started.

"Kamal as I requested everyone, please don't feel offended. The open door is moreover a practice, not a policy. Technically policy is a rule-set and most of the time coupled with the regulation and compliances, for example, maternity or the paternity benefits. Up to a large extent, it remains the same across the organizations. Whereas practice is an activity one keeps doing for improvement. It will be different when exercised by the different people, may differ depending on the organization's culture."

"So what you are doing as the open door is a practice, to help people and bring more transparency," I asked Kamal.

"Reaching out to a leader is a tough thing to do for people. One has to cross through the visible (like secretory or office assistant) and invisible barrier, that separates the leader from the outside world. People feel difficult to interrupt their leader whatever they're doing and then tell them something unpleasant. Nobody wants to do that." Sodi added his point.

"It's easy to say that I have an open door, come to me with any problems. But try to understand no one wants to be a part of the problem. People don't want to get in a negative image and they are afraid to speak up. Because if things don't go well they will be screwed up. It's like giving them the extra burden to openly communicate their problems or suggestions for improvement, which naturally most people resist. " I said.

"The other problem is when organization's leaders announced the open door policy, it makes them great and feel good at the cost of middle-level management. It encourages employees to bypass their immediate manager whenever they have a complaint to offer or a problem to solve. It's like, to make one employee happy you are making another employee unhappy." Sodi said.

"But nothing is wrong in it, if the immediate manager fails to address the concern then people have the right to reach on next level." One participant intervenes in the discussion.

"Yes, you are absolutely right, people should reach any level if their problem doesn't get resolved. But are you developing the culture of open-door practice across the organization or only specific people are promoting this? If it is specific to the people, then many of the other leaders may not even get the opportunity to listen and address the concern of their team members as their bosses are already encouraging people in the name of an open-door to bypass them. It works effectively if the chain of command is honored." I said.

"And I have another point, why people have to reach out to their leaders. Today is the time of servant leadership where leaders should reach to their people to understand their challenges and concerns. Looking out for the problems is not the same as seeing the problem. When leaders proactively approach their people, it makes them comfortable to share their concerns." Sodi added his views and continued speaking.

"Believe me or not, but I strongly believe when leaders expect that people visit their cabin to share their frustration or concerns, it won't happen at the leader's place. The leader's place is always a power center, the atmosphere won't allow the candidate to speak out. So go out at cafeteria, meeting room or any informal places if you want to listen to your people."

"I think we have great inputs on the open door practice, do we want to continue the discussion or move to the next challenges. I hope Kamal this should give you some insight to overcome your challenge with open door" Jignesh intervened as the first topic was getting stretched, he is a great moderator.

Yes, we should move to the next question and I got interesting observations, thanks, everyone." Kamal said.

"So next is Mr. Amandeep Saxena, who is working as COO in Fintech Company and he is in the States from the last 12 years working on various leadership profiles. Amandeep now over to you." Jignesh Bhai called on the next candidate to share their challenges.

"Thanks, Jignesh for your efforts in organizing such a session. I like the format of open discussion, the previous discussion was very useful and I was not aware of the other sight of an open-door policy. I was also thinking of everyone else having another star on their badge by having an open door policy. And we all are in the same boat and sharing problems and exchanging the experience and learning if we can improve a bit, nothing like it. Once again thank you, Nikhil and Vikas, you are amazing." Amandeep was very excited, and such excitement is the immediate feedback of any session. So I was happy and in big relief that it's going in the right direction.

"Thanks, Amandeep for your nice words and sharing the feedback. Let's start with your challenge." Jignesh Bhai asked him, he was committed to maintaining the time frame.

"Ya sure, my challenge is a common issue and I am sure that everyone in leadership profile face it. People are good and dedicated but they lack accountability, How do I build accountability in people? Does anyone also has a similar challenge?" Amandeep asked the group.

Another person stood up "Yes, I take care of my team, I am always accommodating with their demands, never shout on them, in totality I do whatever is required, but fail to understand what else I can do to get them accountable."

One another participant jumped into the discussion and added "creating a culture of accountability is tough, even you can't provide the feedback on team mistake, and they see you as a villain. How do I provide constructive feedback without being a bad person? " Looks like everyone is facing this challenge, the discussion would be interesting.

It didn't end here, another person said, "How can I hold a team member to be held accountable and still be seen as a good leader?"

"In the end, we are accountable either to management or the clients. If our team is not supporting us by taking accountability for their part, how can we fulfill our commitment. As a leader, our commitments are depending on the team members." Amandeep added.

"I think we have enough on the problem statement, let's start our discussion to find the solution." Jignesh Bhai interrupted before anyone else can start repeating the same problem.

"Let me ask you some questions, and you don't need to reply but to introspect. These are the key rules for leaders to be followed before expecting accountability. Yes as a leader you are responsible and unless your team members don't support you, your commitments are bound to fail. As a leader, you might be doing so many things and trying to become a role model by taking on more and more responsibilities but I have seen many leaders fail to understand why their team members aren't willing to take accountability. It is known as 'Cognitive Bias' in which leaders start assuming that other people think the same way that they do. Due to this assumption, leaders fail to set the correct expectations and start expecting accountability." I said.

"But my commitment and dedication towards my work and organization are not sufficient for others to understand that similarly, they should be accountable. Are they not seeing I am working day and night?" Now Amandeep looks frustrated.

"I can understand your challenge, first of all, the biggest problem in setting accountability is 'I' and 'they'. You and your team are not the South Pole and the North Pole, unless you and your team members are not on the same side, a culture of accountability cannot be developed." Sodi said.

"You always need to think that you are a part of the team like everyone is in the same boat. In a team, people get connected, if they feel they are an equal partner, the only difference between them is that everyone carries different responsibilities. If you choose the other side 'I', then people will hesitate in taking responsibility. They will always look forward to you taking every responsibility. But if you make them realize that you all are in the same court, then responsibilities will be easily shared." I said with strong conviction.

"It's a different perspective of how one can think about the team and be a part of it. Although it looks like a very small thing when you are given the example of court, it was an eye-opener for me. Leader and their team cannot be on a different side of the court. Due to this, they might be reluctant in taking ownership. But my question is, what is the thing which holds people to take accountability?" One of the participants added his views.

"There are many other factors which make people apprehensive about taking accountability, not just this one. In my opinion, it's all depending on the leader's behavior which enables people to take ownership." I said.

"Another key factor is communication, how effectively leaders are communicating their expectations to team members. The clearer they are, the more team member will be willing to take responsibility. Unclarity in expectation holds people from taking ownership. Because they always fear if they are not able to meet the expectation of the leader due to the unclarity, there will be negative consequences. No one wants to be in problem, so they feel safe by avoiding the ownership of work." I said and continued speaking.

"Many leaders never take the accountability of communicating with their expectations clearly, decisions, and action plans if their team members fail to meet. They always see the problem in people. Hence people afraid of taking accountability due to the inability of their leaders' communication skills. As a leader, you should listen first and speak last."

"That's amazing insight, Nikhil, I never imagined that communication plays such a role in making people accountable." Jignesh Bhai was impressed, and I know him even if he is not impressed but always encourages others.

"Thanks, Jignesh Bhai, another challenge is whether leaders are taking accountability for their decisions or not. This is another key factor, anyone won't be serious about taking accountability if they see their leaders are not serious about their actions and decisions. People learn from their leaders, leadership is waterfall practice what you are setting at the top will flow down at the below level. Many leaders and managers want their team members to be punctual at reaching the office on time but they hardly follow. Because they don't obey their own decision of coming office on time, they make stringent process and system to punish the employees who fail to comply. Then how you can think that they will take accountability." I said.

Sodi said "Let me add one more point apart from the communication and respecting own decisions. Another important factor is constructive feedback. If leaders see that there is a problem with their people in taking accountability, they are afraid of giving constructive feedback. Either they just blame and shout or don't say anything, but none of the approaches helps people taking accountability. Just give the people feedback but it should not be **What they haven't done** rather it should **What was the gap and how they can do it?** Unfortunately, many leaders just want to avoid the confrontation by their team members, which they may face while giving the feedback."

Everybody started clapping, looks like everyone is enjoying the discussion. Initially, most of the people were apprehensive but as the discussion was moving everyone was trying to participate.

But it looks like Amandeep has still some questions, he said: "Thanks to everyone for such insight, still I am looking for the remedy to build the accountability among the team."

Jignesh Bhai was looking confused about whether to take this discussion further or to jump on the next topic. So he asked the people "Shall we continue with this discussion to understand the remedy or move on to the new topic." And everyone responded in the same voice that we want to listen to some solution. "Okay, it's a democracy and the majority wins. So Nikhil and Vikas over to you. Let us know what we can do to develop a culture of accountability. "

"First of all, as a leader, we should not mix personal and team accountability, both are different things. As a leader, it's your job to provide them with a definition of what it is that you're holding them accountable for, this will help in improving accountability." I started answering the solution.

"Before expecting or assuming anything leader should ask themselves about the **Whys**, why are you expecting? Why your team is coming to the office? Why they are being given any project or assignment? Spend time with your team members to make them understand why they need to spend their time doing what you are expecting. Why does it matter for them? We always tend to tell people what to do; many leaders are good at that. Remember it's not 'what', it's the **Whys** which connects the people because **Why** gives a purpose and **What is** just **a task to do."** I started explaining the solution, it's a five 'C' concept to build accountability among the team members, **where first 'C' is a "common" purpose.**

"The next step is setting clear expectations. What do you want to achieve? What is the outcome are you expecting, it should be in black and white words, and should be repeated as many times as it is required unless your team doesn't get the clarity on what is expected from them? It takes time, sometimes you may feel tiring in repetition but don't hold back until the entire team can communicate them effectively." **This was my second 'C' for "clarity".**

Sodi intervenes, "I agree with Nikhil. Don't be shy in clarifying the thing. As a leader, it's your key responsibility. Just setting the expectation for example that 'I need a solution to a problem by the evening' is not giving clarity to the team. I still say it's a vague thing."

"Sorry, Mr. Sodi what you are saying is contradicting with Mr. Nikhil's solution, now I am confused, you mean to say even after setting the correct expectation as per your example it is a vague thing. Then what are you expecting leaders to do?" One young man interrupted Sodi.

Sodi smiled and responded, "I heard you, gentlemen. What's your name?"

"I am Aakash, working as Chief Customer Officer with a consulting firm." The young enthusiastic replied.

"Great Aakash, let me clarify your confusion. As a leader one is not supposed to give a single liner statement and expect people will take the accountability to fulfill their expectations. That's never happening. One statement 'I need a solution by the evening of a problem' can be interpreted in multiple ways. Are you looking for one specific viable solution to a problem, or are you asking the team to jointly agree on multiple potential solutions to present? Do you expect them to define a roadmap for one or multiple solutions, or not? Do you need them to present a list of pros and cons with their solution(s)? How do you want to be kept informed along the way? By a weekly update every Friday via email or status update meeting on every Monday or what? Unless the leader brings a deep level of clear expectations, it can't be met. Just giving a statement and assuming the rest of the things won't help you to get what you are expecting?" Sodi said in one flow, everyone was amazed looks like they never thought that just setting the expectation by a single liner is not enough it requires detailing. "Nikhil, you can continue," Sodi asked me.

"Thanks, Sodi, for adding a beautiful example to make all of us understand how and up to what level clarity is important. Once you have clarified the 'why' it means purpose and set the correct expectations, don't just sit and relax. As time passes, it's a leader's job to keep a team focused and aligned so that everyone's involved and moving in the same direction. How are they going to do what you need them to do? What resources might they consider using? Keep everyone focused. Over and over, communicate with them, ask questions, and remind them why and what they're doing is important. Your job as a leader is to keep them all rowing in the same direction, especially when rolling out long-term plans. Communication and alignment are key things that provide direction to any team because it fosters long-term sustainability." **That's my third 'C' for "communication".**

"Now the next stage comes for the leaders to monitor and review the progress. It's not about micromanaging the team but regular monitoring helps you identify the gaps and areas of improvement, don't tell them what to do. Coach them. Be a resource for them. What roadblocks need to be removed, and how can you help remove them?" **The fourth 'C' is for "collaboration"** and "coaching" are the key areas where leaders get the opportunity to nurture and converse with their team members. Coaching is a game analogy where the coach never plays but makes sure that he or she is doing all that is required for his/her team to win. True leaders are a coach who mentors their team to succeed.

I noticed that everyone is just listening, there was hardly any reaction or response. I thought is it an overdose of stretching one issue for so long or people are listening so silently with great interest that they don't want to miss any point?

"Hey everyone, are you following me?" I asked the audience.

"Yess!" without a second of delay everyone said in one voice. It was amazing, people are taking an interest and it's a quick appreciation for any speaker. Now I want to disclose to them the last 'C' of building accountability with the team.

"There is one more practice which leader need to incorporate religiously to make people understand about the accountability is to share the consequences if they aren't willing to take accountability" before I continue someone standup and said.

"But sharing consequences is like giving a threat to team members, thus it's a negative thing. With such practice how one can build trust and get the accountable people?"

"True I like your attentiveness. That's the issue, most people see consequences and they immediately think of a negative connotation. We overlook that such consequences can also be positive. Make results and consequences visible, it always inspires people. If people have the visibility of what ultimately they are going to achieve if they take accountability, then, for sure they will own the things. As a leader, you have to share consequences strategically and tactically, share it like a goal, and sometimes even if you have to share the negative consequences, you should share with them. People will understand it and act accordingly. But if you are not sharing how will they be able to help you? Just sharing the negative outcome and blaming the team that didn't do well, won't help any leader. How you can expect your team to take care of something of which they are not aware. That is from my side." I finished my theory of building accountability with **last and fifth 'C' of "consequences".**

Amandeep stood and join the hand in a *namaste* position (An Indian gesture out of respect) and bow down his head. *"Sir Ji Tussi great ho, Tofa Kabul Karo* (A famous dialogue from an Indian movie, 'You are great, please accept my gesture')" And started clapping and everyone in the room joined him. It was a fantastic moment.

"Nikhil I never thought so deeply that it's a leader's accountability to make their team accountable and if a team is not accountable, then it's a gap in leadership not with the people. What an acumen you have, I have gone through many leadership programs and read many books but never got such a level of insight. Thanks for sharing." Amandeep said and I can sense a true thank from his voice.

Now it's Jignesh Bhai's turn to taking the discussion on a new topic. "Thanks, everyone, no doubt about Nikhil but all learnings are coming because everyone is open. Thanks for a great collaboration in this session. Shall we move to another question?" And everyone said in one voice. All were very excited about what next.

One young champ stood up and gave his introduction. His name was Vinay and was working with Product Development Company as a Product Head. He shared "Whenever we have any issue in our company our Chief Product Architect either starts making a new process or initiate a new training. We already have a lot of processes in place and it's constantly increasing, like compound interest. Now, whenever any challenges or issues come we don't get afraid of facing and resolving them but our threat is one more process, series of meetings, and useless training will start. Why do leaders love so many processes? "

Sodi jumped in and said, *"Vinay you sound like Problem se dar nahi lagata saheb par process se lagta hai* (Not afraid from the problem but from the process which comes out of the problem)." And everyone was laughing at Sodi's humorous touch.

When Jignesh Bhai asked the audience for more input another person added, "Yes I also experienced the same thing. Many times I feel, am

I just working for the processes? Truly speaking the majority of time core areas are kept aside."

"Processes are important and they are made to help people. I always say processes are meant for people, people are not meant for processes. Unfortunately, many leaders over a period start focusing more on the process rather than the problem. They feel the solution to every problem resides in the process. I am not denying that up to some extent it is true. But in any condition process cannot bypass the people. Leaders have to see if their people are spending more time on maintaining the processes as compared to their core areas then it's a process problem. If processes are not helping team members to improve their productivity or simplify their day-to-day problem then your process is not working at all." I said.

"True Nikhil, it's a vicious circle of creating process, then giving training for them and doing review meeting, and if it creates a new problem rather solving the previous one, the leaders create a new process and the cycle continues. But why do leaders love the process so much?" Vinay said.

"Any process generates some or other statistics or data and when the leader gets it, it gives them the feeling of control or opportunity to make an opinion out of it. This helps them to justify why the problem occurred and how they are going to control that problem in the future. I am not saying it is always a bad thing, but when a leader becomes the Messiah and starts projecting that the root cause of any problem is always an absence of process and they have fixed that problem by inventing a new process then I have a strong objection. The solution to every problem is not a process, there are many other reasons like management style, skills, capabilities, funds, organization reputation etc, there is an endless list."

"In one of the IT Service Company, an owner was keen to take any work order even if they don't have the required skills. He believed that once you jump in a river you will learn to swim automatically. But that's not the case, some may survive but most of the people will die. Even if they survive, they will not thrive. But his approach didn't work and almost in every case customer started complaining about the poor quality of work. He blamed the project manager for not having the learning process in place and to solve the problem he decided for project managers to buy the course from Udemy to learn so they can get trained. Managers followed the approach but failed to understand how to identify if their people are trained or not. Again the CEO becomes the Messiah and suggested having the review meeting to know about their learning. And it kept going. The problem was not solved, as the root cause was not the process, it was the skill. It doesn't matter what level of the well-articulated process you have but if you don't have the right people to implement there won't be any result. So the leader should focus on people not on the process. " I finished my response asked Sodi if he wants to add anything.

"I completely agree with you, Nikhil. Whenever a business gets in trouble, the first thing leaders want to do is invent a new process. They think that more emphasis on the process will make them more efficient. The truth is that the ad-hoc process usually does more harm than good. This rarely solves the problems and is intended to cause such havoc that it often takes a business time to recover. When it's all over, the underlying problems remain, but time, momentum, and credibility have been lost." Sodi added.

"Does this answer your question?" Jignesh Bhai asked the audience and looks like everyone was good with that. He said now we are left with 30 minutes, so need to quickly wrap up, I would request the audience to ask about more common issues so everyone can get benefited and will also request our expert to provide a short answer. I am sorry for it, but we have a time crunch." Jignesh Bhai was in a hurry now.

"I am grateful to be a part of this session today. My name is Yuvraj, without wasting time in giving the background and personal introduction I am going to directly jump on my question. Based on the discussion what I have understood is that leaders have to spend more time with their team to coach and collaborate with them. But most of the leaders are so occupied they don't get the time for their people. If leadership requires such a level of effort and time then organizations have to think about offloading their responsibilities. I just wanted to ask the audience to raise their hand if you want to hear something on this issue." And the majority of people agreed with Yuvraj about the busyness of their leaders.

"Many leaders like to talk about how busy they are. That's the problem. Mostly, it is an effort to signal importance. If any leader constantly feels the need to show that they have a million better things to be paying attention to than what's going on in front of them, then at the very least that leaders are seriously confused about their priorities."

"The truth is that there's nothing worse than a constantly busy leader. First, it tells people around that they are not so important. Second, it limits the leader's visibility and awareness. If leaders are busy all the time, how can they know what's going on?"

"The truth is that leaders who say they're busy usually just can't get things done. They confuse activity for action, rudeness for importance, and status for success. It's possible to be busy for a day or even a week, but if they are always busy, either you're doing something very wrong or just fooling yourself." I said and asked Sodi to add his views.

"I'm busy. It's a compulsion for many leaders to say, otherwise, they feel people will not consider them as an important person who carries the load of the organization. For many, if we aren't busy, then we aren't important, right?" Sodi asked the audience and some nodded or some were clueless and he continued.

"When the leader gives a reason of busyness and don't spend time with people in solving problems, coaching or listening to them, in my view its nothing but it's an unfair treatment by the leaders to their people. For any leader, people cannot be a second priority. And if the people are not being treated fairly by their leaders, then they won't help their colleagues and won't be among the best performers in the company. People reach to leaders as they have a dependency on them for getting the direction, suggestion, decisions, opinion, and input. The busyness of the leader becomes an obstacle in people's growth and if people are not growing under the leader then what is the purpose of leadership." Sodi finished his comment on the busyness of leaders.

"Thanks, Sodi and Nikhil for your great inputs. In my view, all this comes when leaders have an attitude of 'doing things in my way'. They are adamant about their approach and not flexible enough to listen to what their people want or you can say they fail to learn from them about their expectations. Can you highlight why this happens? Why do leaders fail to understand such a small thing? As we are left with few minutes, so it would be great to close the session by putting some light on it." Jignesh Bhai summarizes the previous discussion and smartly drives the session to an end but with a very good question.

"It's a great question, Jignesh Bhai. What I have learned and experienced that it is pseudo leadership. The majority of people want to become a leader so they can have control over a people, they can command others, and they can give instruction and can make followers who believe in their showoffs. And all problem starts from here, such a leader who wants people should take an interest in them, but they are not interested in people. This leads to having a very weak or no relationship with people. Because to nurture the relationship or to understand people one has to invest time and efforts. Unfortunately, pseudo leaders don't have the time they are always busy and carry all other priorities than people. They expect that people will come to them, but they won't reach out to them."

I continued "And in the name of fostering the relationship they celebrate birthdays, play ping pong, do outdoor parties, and assume to have a strong relationship. But they forget free beer or food doesn't bring commitment. They forget that people are looking for growth and opportunities, everyone has some or other goals. Unless leaders don't have a strong relationship with people, they are not going to share their goals. If the leader doesn't know what people want, then how he/she can align themselves with organization's goals."

"Relations can make or break an organization. Synergic team relations will make a business successful in the long run. A good understanding between people and leaders is important to reduce any conflicts. It acts as a catalyst for the success of any organization. A positive relationship between both of them leads to higher motivation and team engagement. When people are happy, they are more productive. They will put more effort into their work, and this translates into satisfied customers and ultimately brings more revenue to your business."

"People are at the center of all leadership efforts. Leaders cannot lead unless they understand the people they are leading. Besides, that weak relationship doesn't have the trust and confidence in leadership and without trust and confidence, one leader can't drive to achieve the goals."

"The other biggest problem in the current competitive business arena is that good financial results and metrics are often the main determinants of a company or a leader's strength. This defines a 'metrics-driven business culture and leadership. I am not denying the importance of data, it does help leaders by providing a better way of managing, monitoring, and tracking to bring an improvement. But developing a relationship with people cannot be driven by the data, it has to be nurtured. What distinguishes a great leader from a good leader is the person's ability to foster deep-rooted and trustworthy connections with the people they work with."

"That's what I have to share, Jignesh Bhai, time is also over. But I must say it was one of the wonderful sessions I have ever attended. Great format, kudos to you and your team for organizing such an interesting event." I quickly concluded.

Thereafter Sodi and some participants also gave their views, feedback, and thank you notes. But overall people enjoyed the session and they are looking forward to having more similar interactions. We all chit-chatted for the next 10-15 minutes and left the venue. While coming back I was thinking it is very easy to become or declare yourself a leader but it takes efforts and time to establish. If your intent is just controlling the people then you're not a leader, you are a control freak?

Check out the following question, to determine if you are a control freak or a leader?

- Are you a leader just because of the title or position?
- Have you ever taken any coaching before pursuing a leadership profile?
- Do you think it is important for a leadership profile that people are reporting to you?
- Can someone be a leader without any title?
- Do you think it's people's responsibility to follow the leader?
- Does creating a new process give you satisfaction irrespective of the process is achieving its goal or not?
- Do you have a clear distinction between policy and practice in your organization?
- Have you been able to draw the desired results through an open-door policy?
- Have you faced challenges in holding your team members accountable?
- Do you think the only process in place is enough?
- Have you experienced that presence of too many processes is becoming a challenge?
- Does your team give you challenges in following processes?
- Does your team complain about processes?
- Is finding time for your team a challenge for you?

"The key to successful leadership is influence not authority"
-Kenneth Blanchard

10

Hum Nahin Sudharenge

LEADER'S INABILITY TO LEARN FROM FAILURES

"When leaders fail to learn from the failures and makes repeated mistakes"

It's been my habit since the start of my firm that I occasionally take out the whole team or some members for lunch now and then. Today Avantika was busy with her work so I relieved her from preparing the lunch for me as I had to go out.

I called upon Aashutosh, "Hey, buddy, what's your plan for lunch," I asked.

"Nothing special boss," Aashutosh replied, he has a habit of calling me boss. Although I don't like it when he says I feel like a friend is teasing me.

"Great, join me. We are going out for lunch."I invited him.

"Is it with some client, boss?"He threw one more question.

"*Naa* (no) just you and me. Now hurry up, let's go" I got up from my chair.

After some time we were in a good and quiet place with great ambiance in the corner of a restaurant. After ordering lunch I asked "*Aur kya chal raha hai, Aashutosh* (How is everything Aashutosh)."

"Nothing much boss," He replied but his voice was not very convincing.

"Tell me we have time before the food arrives."I insisted.

"Boss I wanted to ask you a question that has been troubling me for days."He hesitantly said.

"Ohh come on Aashutosh, shoot what is troubling you."I tried to make him at ease.

"Boss we have been consulting a lot of the organization and we found that most and most of them are struggling because of leadership issues. The more we dig deeper we find that the root cause lies somewhere in the leadership and that is ok but what I have observed is that these leaders keep on committing the same mistakes over and over again." Aashutosh said that in one breath.

"Yes, that is rightly observed but what is the question that's troubling you."I was trying to figure out the question.

"My question is why for god's sake leaders don't learn from their mistakes and keep on committing them over and over again."Aashutosh sounded frustrated.

"Hahaha...Aashutosh you really scared me for a moment. Your question is very innocent on one hand but at the same time, you have hit the bull's eye. For one thing, I must appreciate that you are thinking in the right direction and that is very good. Now coming to your question let me try to answer that before our meal comes."

"I continued, "See Aashutosh everyone makes mistakes, and leaders are no exception to it. The only difference is when a leader makes a mistake the stakes are high and the whole team pays for it".

"Many of the times mistakes made by leaders result in failures but that too is a natural phenomenon in the path to success. The people who learn from their mistakes especially leaders, and make the right amends, eventually succeed and that adds to their experience which has been shared with and benefited by the team as well."

"But boss my question was why a leader keeps on committing the same mistake and fails to learn from them."Aashutosh interrupted.

"I am coming to that point . You see it is very simple that a leader should identify the mistakes early on and most importantly not repeat them but why a leader keeps on committing the same mistakes repeatedly, it leads to the failure of the whole organization. Is that what bothering you?"

"Yes, boss exactly." Aashutosh has now leaned forward and listened carefully.

"Let me try to explain it to you in very simple terms. The two most common reasons I came across are, first, these leaders are too much convinced with their ideas, way of working, and approach, that they just refuse to admit that they might be doing it in the wrong way. These leaders invest so much time in investigating the cause of failure and finally convince themselves that the problem lies somewhere else and they are doing everything right."

"Let me give you an example. It was before you joined, we were consulting a firm. Mr. Rawat was the CEO and was also leading the Sales team of the organization by himself. He was drawing results along with the team and made the firm a success. But as time passed his sales strategies became obsolete and required some revisits in approach. It was high time to introduce some new tactics and methods to his strategies provided that the market, as well as the nature of the client, was changing rapidly."

"The sales figure started to decline lower and lower. The potentials were not turning into clients and the existing clients started to leave. It was an alarming situation in the organization. All the stakeholders were very furious because the organization was derailing from its path of success as the numbers indicated. They had all the faith in Mr. Rawat so they left it to him to fix whatever the problem was."

"But on the contrary, Mr. Rawat was convinced that he is doing it all right and there is nothing wrong with his strategies as they had given results in the past. He thought at that time that the problem lies with the team. They must have not executed strategy exactly as they were told to do. So he started micromanaging on how to do the things, about the processes and procedures but nothing worked. This lead to frustration due to the continuous decrease in sales and revenue which ultimately required some bold actions."

"Did Mr. Rawat approach you? Did he realize it's time to seek a coach?"Aashutosh asked enthusiastically. "Ha-ha-ha. No, on the contrary, he fired some guys from his sales team. "I replied.

"Really, are you serious boss?"Ashutosh was in shock.

"You bet I am."

"Then what happened," Aashutosh asked.

"More failure resulted in more firing. Even some good performing salespeople from other organizations with a proven track record were hired but failed miserably under Rawat's leadership resulting in their departure too."

"After that Mr. Rawat must have realized his mistakes, I am sure."Aashutosh passed a judgment and laid back waiting for my approval.

"My boy you are wrong again."

"Whatttt?"Ashutosh's eyes were wide open.

"Yes Aashutosh, the conclusion Mr. Rawat reached, after a very deep retrospect was that he is not able to recruit the right man who can just simply do as instructed. He has all the plans and strategies sorted out but was not able to get the right guys to implement and execute. The decrease in the revenue continued and the organization was almost collapsed when they hired us."

"What happened to the organization afterward?" Aashutosh asked.

"They are doing very well now but it required a lot of coaching and mentoring. You see in this case only if Rawat would have dared to admit that it's time to make a shift in his approach and strategies, he and only the organization might have saved themselves from having a rough patch, but Mr. Rawat was so much convinced by the fact that what he knew was the best way, he didn't allow himself to be flexible enough to make the shift and moreover, the baggage of the past success also played a culprit in this case."

"Hmmm, now I can see. Boss, he was not having the courage to admit that he was committing a mistake was the problem there, you earlier said two common reasons what the other one is?" - Aashutosh.

"Looks like our food is also taking more time than expected so we can continue with our discussion. The second reason where a leader keeps on committing and repeating mistakes as it is often seen in the organization, that where the leader surrounds himself with the 'yes' man and enjoys their praises. On the other hand, straight and honest feedback is not welcomed."

"Do you remember any such example boss?"Aashutosh asked.

"I do, in fact many" I replied with a witty smile.

"Please share?"Aashutosh looked excited.

"I have an interesting case to share, we came across this company during one of our assignments, you might have heard about it from any of your colleagues. As I could remember it was before your joining. There was a midsize company and the owner's name was Gopikrishnan, he used to make all the strategic decisions of his organization. As usual, some of the decisions were not proved to be the best ones and didn't draw the desired results."

Gopikrishnan being a good leader always held retrospective meetings (A retrospective is a meeting held after work is done to discuss what happened during the execution of work, intending to improve things in the future based on those learnings and conversations. It's a popular term in Agile Methodology) of his decisions which did not work well with the core team. The intentions were very good and he was doing the right thing but as it is said that good intentions are the *pathway to hell (The road to hell* is paved with good intentions means that it is not enough to simply mean to do well, one must take action to do well). The result comes if the execution is correct not necessarily the intention."

"But in reality, things were happening differently, not as Gopikrishnan was assuming. He used to invite the team to share their honest assessment, his most trusted and favorite sales head Kanahiya Kumar used to come for his praising and defended his decision by all his strength overpowering all the straight and honest feedback, making Mr. Gopikrishnan believe that there was nothing wrong with the decision but somehow for other reasons it didn't work."

"It was not so that the honest opinion was not shared with Gopikrishnan by other team members but it was not considered and not paid due attention as Kanahiya always defended his decisions in front of him and other team members."

"Here those people who are giving straight and honest feedback, take a back seat with the fear of being disliked or fall in the bad books of a leader. And it's a very common and natural tendency among the employees."

"That's why a leader is required to take a lot of effort to make a culture of safe environment and freedom at least with the core team where the assessment or the retrospective meetings can take place in the true sense. Otherwise, it will give a very false satisfaction to the leader of doing the assessment or retrospect meeting but not getting the desired outcome. They just remain a fancy word or fancy processes in an organization which looks very appealing and impressive from outside but hollow in practice."

"It resulted in drifting away from all the other team members from telling the truth. Slowly and gradually all the voices went silent and people like Kanahiya Kumar prevailed and kept rising the ladder . It impacted the organization badly in due course. The people who took the courage of sharing the honest opinion witnessed Kanahiya Kumar's success and that gave them a sense of either being silent or join the band of praises with Kanahiya Kumar."

"The leader must always keep in mind that the employee sitting on the highest ranks of the organization will not risk his career growth if they have a feeling that highlighting the mistake of the leader may jeopardize their job or growth. It's the leader's responsibility to give that confidence to the team very deliberately and timely. It's an ongoing process that requires more actions than words."

"In this case, Gopikrishnan always encouraged honest and straight feedback but failed to reflect that in actions. He also failed to nurture this in practice as well as to create a culture of honest feedback in the organization. Just declaring is not enough but you have to practice it yourself".

"Once a CEO asked me why people fear from telling the truth, and giving me a straight feedback when I ask. I always encourage them to do so, I never get angry, I replied to him that have you seen your facial reactions when some of your employees give you feedback?

Yes!!! Your team notices your body language."

"So as you have seen it happens both ways sometimes the leader doesn't admit mistakes and sometimes people around them don't allow them to. Hence, they keep on making the same mistakes again and again."

"Oh yes, Nikhil this seems to be the most prominent reasons among many others. But I strongly believe learning from the mistakes, gaps and failure is an opportunity for a leader" Aashutosh said.

"True Aashutosh, Failure is the most powerful source for know-how and understanding. It teaches you about survival, renewal, and reinvention of yourself and the organization that you are leading. Whether it's a decision any leaders make, the people they hire, the investment they make, the relationship they have nurtured from each experience, they have the opportunity to learn something new about leadership."

"Failure is one of life's greatest sources of learning. As a leader, if you never failed at anything, you would never be forced to take action to course-correct or try new ways to encash opportunities that you never know until a failure happens. In the end, it's what you do with failure that defines your character as a leader. For example, do you admit failure or do you find a creative way to hide reality? Do you ask yourself what you learned during the process of failing – or do you hold someone else accountable and/or blame the circumstances you were faced with to deflect criticism of the failed outcome?"

"Great leadership is about being accountable for your actions. Some of the greatest leaders in history failed at one time or another, a list that includes Bill Gates, Steve Jobs, Thomas Edison, Walt Disney, and many others. Their ability to hold themselves accountable enabled them to persevere, become better leaders, and build their legacies."

"Great leaders don't run away or mask their failure, they confront the issue from the front and evaluate what they could have done better, and introspect on the lessons learned. They ask their team members to provide feedback and identify the opportunities that can be seized from this learning moment."

"Let me share one of my failures Aashutosh, in the initial days of my career in the States I was responsible for losing one of the key accounts that cost the company $7 million in annual revenue. At that time, my leadership style was too relaxed and casual depending on others rather than being proactive about making the system better. This failure forced me to find ways to make the system more effective and interdependent upon the decisions made by each departmental leader. The process of reinventing the system made our team stronger and more united. We all got matured and designed an entirely new set of best practices that renewed our entire business model and approach; this allowed us to acquire new accounts and became a much more innovative team."

"That's a fantastic example, although it's a hard pill to swallow that you have faced failures" Aashutosh replied.

"No one is perfect Aashutosh, we all do mistakes. The most important thing is we should be mature enough to learn from the mistakes. Failure makes leaders stronger and wiser, once this attitude is developed they become fearless and empowered to trust their gut and thus enable themselves to make better decisions. Failure helps a leader to foresee risk and challenges beforehand which ensures that they are not far away from success. Once leaders take the time to reflect upon what they could have done to avoid failure, it puts them in a position of strength that allows trusting their instincts. This also allows leaders to be more resourceful with their relationships. It enables their entrepreneurial spirit as a leader and they can begin to see opportunities with greater clarity and focus."

Aashutosh replied "Nikhil, I can correlate with Hindi proverb *'Aapda main Avsar'* (Every problem has an opportunity). Failure is not a bad thing. It is a wake-up call for the next opportunity. Many leaders forget that opportunity is the mother of success and second chance is around them. With this lens, failure allows leaders to see opportunities with broader observation."

"Well said, Aashutosh". The waiter arrived with our food. "Now time to feed the stomach, we should not fail to enjoy this tasty food". Then I and Aashutosh continued to discuss why leaders hesitate to learn from failure while having lunch.

• • • • • •

Are you also a leader who is afraid of learning from failures, if yes then checkout the following questions.

- Have you ever hesitated to admit your mistakes in front of your team?
- Have you encouraged your team to come up and highlight your mistakes? Have you coached your team to do that constructively?

- Have you faced challenges in giving your team the confidence to share their honest feedback?
- Do you have all the intention to give your team the freedom to speak their minds in front of you but don't know how to do it?
- Are you surrounded by 'yes sir/mam' but don't know how to deal with them?
- Have you faced challenges in striking a balance between straightforward and 'yes sir/mam' employees?

"The only real mistake is the one from which we learn nothing"

-Kenneth Blanchard

11

Seth Ji Ki Mandali

LEADERS NURTURING NEPOTISM

"When leaders kill the right talent due to their preferences, trustworthiness, insecurities, or just for self-pleasing"

What happened Avantika you look very upset? Is everything all right?"For the last 2-3 days, I noticed Avantika is tensed. I was also very busy due to the audits happening in the office, so didn't get the time to pay full attention.

"Ya, everything is okay, Nikhil, but that's true I am very upset," Avantika replied without any energy. I rarely see her with less energy, she always carries momentum and charm in life.

"So can I know what is bothering my sweetheart?" I was now concerned.

"Are you not following the news coming from India?" Avantika was surprised.

"You know dear I rarely follow the desi news, so tell me what happened in our country?" Avantika has a habit of constantly watching the news whether it's from India or the US, and many times she gets upset. Nowadays channels are not sharing the news, they inject their agendas. One of my favorite Bollywood stars passed away, Sushant Singh Rajput", she said in a very sad tone.

"Oh, I am so sorry about that, but I am also sorry as I am not able to recall him. Does he belong to the younger generation?"

Actually, from the last couple of years, I lost interest in watching movies as other priorities increased over a period otherwise I never leave a chance to watch them and when you are in the US it's a common way to get connected with India.

"How come you don't know about Sushant Singh, he was a rising star in India. Do you remember MS Dhoni's movie, we watched with Aashutosh in AMC theatre." Avantika said.

"Yes, I remember, it was a classic movie."

"Sushant played the role of Dhoni," - Avantika.

"Oh, that's really bad what happened to him, he was quite young." I was wondering how someone can pass away at such a young age.

"He committed suicide", she replied.

"What??" I was surprised, "Why did he take such a step?"

"He committed suicides due to nepotism spread across Bollywood," Avantika replied with some anger.

"What is this nonsense Avantika, he has done many big movies and has been successful so how can you say he gave away his life due to nepotism." I didn't agree with this thought at all.

"Nikhil, check any news channel or social media everyone is saying it is due to nepotism. The industry is controlled by some top shots like superstars or production houses and they decide the fate of any newcomer. They wrote the fate of Sushant Singh, and so he was forced to do suicide. " – Avantika.

"Avantika, whatever has happened is sad. But I disagree with this fact. I have less belief in media they run their agenda to get TRPs (A television rating system), for them, it's a business. They just set the narrative, many times whatever we see from our eyes that even isn't true. And no need to talk about social media, that is a jungle where people are free to say anything, it's complete nonsense. In my opinion, public personalities have more responsibilities as many people follow them, they consider them as a role model. If they take such a step, many people will believe it's the right thing to do and for any small problem of life rather than the fighting spirit, they may also follow the same path. Whatever your conditions are, one must fight." I am always against the giving up approach.

"Nikhil, I agree with your thought of fighting spirit, but we can't imagine how much he was struggling to grow in his career. Nepotism culture was ruining his career." - Avantika.

"Avantika, I was not expecting such thoughts from you, and tell me a place where nepotism doesn't exist. It's everywhere."

"In any industry what else you can expect in the name of nepotism, family and friends of owners joining their business." - Avantika.

"Sorry to say, Avantika then your knowledge is limited, nepotism is not just about owners' family members or friends becoming the part of the company. Nepotism is about killing the right talent in any form by organization's leaders in the name of their preferences, trustworthiness, insecurities, or just for self-pleasing."

She paused for a moment and gave this a thought "True, Nikhil I never thought of this form of nepotism. But why people do it? I can understand their preference for family members or friends but couldn't understand their preference for selective people." -Avantika.

"Avantika, nepotism is deeply rooted in our DNA and centuries' long of practicing it will not and cannot allow for the complete eradication of workplace favoring people close to us. We inherently trust people that are our family and that we consider friends or at least someone known and establishing trust in the workplace environment is one of the crucial elements of doing business successfully."

"So what is the problem?" Avantika.

"The main issue that rises is the favoring of relatives, friends, or anyone else who are not qualified for the given responsibilities. By doing that leaders knowingly or unknowingly are killing the talent."

"But why people will do it if they are not promoting the right talent, the organization will suffer. " - Avantika.

"That's not the case Avantika, the owner or founder of the company places their family members in top positions to ensure their legacy. And this will always be there, you can't get rid away of it. But I am always concerned and very vocal about the other form of nepotism practice followed by the different leaders of organizations which kills more talent as compared to onboarding the owner's family members. That is a more dangerous form of nepotism business."

"Nikhil, you have diverted my mind, now I am curious to understand this different form of nepotism which is nurtured at the workplace."

I was happy to change the mood of Avantika. I continued "This form of nepotism starts with the leader's incapabilities and insecurities, to save their position. They start killing the right talent in an organization that can challenge them. So they promote people who please them and are no threat to their supremacy."

"In one of the organizations, the owner was very close to some of the employees as they were a part of the company when it had started. Their relationship was not just limited to the office, over a period they were doing parties and going out together. This is very normal when you work in a very small group, you tend to develop a close relationship. Besides that during the initial days of business when owners don't have to offer so much, they tried to pacify with such personalized treats and perks."

"As time passes their relationship also becomes closer. Knowingly or unknowingly that relationship takes the shape of nepotism in the organization."

"But how someone's relationship can become nepotism, do you mean to say the owner should not make a good relationship with their team members and especially with the people who did so many sacrifices during the initial day of business?" Avantika made a strong argument, and I knew it, as whenever I had shared this story with anyone, this was the first response I would get.

"No, I am not against if owners or leaders are making the relationship with their people. But every relationship is built out of some reason except the relationship which we get by birth. Let's not get deviated with the definition of a relationship, but why any leader or owner comes in relationship with their people?"

"Can't guess what you are looking for, so you tell me." Avantika.

"The reason for their relationship is to work for that organization. Any leader selects the people with some skills and the purpose is always to contribute to the organization. That's the base of their relationship which is an organization, a post that if they develop a friendship, there is nothing wrong in it, but that should not impact the base for their relationship which is organization. For the sake of their relationship, the organization should not be compromised."

"Unfortunately, that's not the case, leaders and their people cross the thin line of their relationship and damages the organization."

"I am getting what you are saying but still if you can elaborate the example."- Avantika said, looks like my conversation was a heavy dose for her.

"Ya sure, coming back to the example. I came across one company due to some work. It is a perfect example of how a weak owner and his so-called leaders ruin the career of many. The owner aka *Seth Ji* (Owners are called Seth Ji in India out of respect) started the company with some new hires and over a period all of them became friends. The close friend group (employee turned friends) of *Seth Ji* started enjoying the privilege of being close to him. Over a period that privilege put them in a comfort zone, and you know once a person falls in the comfort zone they stop learning, and improving rather they work for survival and do anything and everything for it."

"This entire group become the *'Mandali'* (congregation) and started to worship *Seth Ji* like a king or god and the majority of people enjoy such praising. It's a common phenomenon among many leaders that it's their birthright to be praised as they pay money to the people, they can make or break someone's career. All members of that *'Mandali'* had a mutual understanding that they will make a close shell around the owner so the owner couldn't directly access other people and similarly no other person could access him. Both sides started enjoying this arrangement."

"This relationship impacted the organization so badly that whenever any talented and skilled people joined the organization this *'Mandali'* become active as such people are a threat to their existence. The first thing they did was, not allowing new talented people to get settled in the organization, and most of the time they get to succeed."

"There were instances when some talented people were able to settle in the organization and produced great results and *Seth Ji* started recognizing it. This recognition made *'Mandali'* scared, they started worrying how they will survive as they do nothing and another fear they had was that what would happen if *Seth Ji* changes his expectation and start expecting work from them like new people."

"So when everything fails, 'Shadayantra' (Conspiracy) works, and people from comfort zone are always blessed with these skills.

And one characteristic of *Seth Ji 'Kaan ka Kacha'* (It signifies a person who can be easily misled by an insincere and pretended friend, or just about anyone else who gets to him first with their version of an event or conversation) was adding the fuel to it."

"They prepared all theories, false evidences, manipulated the data, and used to make the wrong presentation in front of *Seth Ji*. They were excellent in making *Seth Ji* realize that you have made the mistake in selecting such people, with their malpractices every time they were able to prove the importance of loyalty over talent. It's not about the talent, it's about loyalty, and when loyalty comes who else is better than us. With a well-designed conspiracy by 'Mandali' some people were kicked off in the name of taking a kickback from the vendor, some were fired with the allegation of they are joining the client, and some in the name of getting benefit from the vendors. These people included all the positions from junior executive to the top level like COO or the operation head. If you see not only these people were the victim of the conspiracies, even unknowingly *Seth Ji* was also a victim. As over a period he lost many talented people, which could have taken organization growth to multifold."

"So this relationship of *Seth Ji* with his *'Mandali'* is one form of the nepotism, which has killed many careers and harassed many talented people. Many leaders develop such *'Mandalis'* of sycophant over a period and they are not able to think beyond the people grouped in *'Mandalis'* and these sycophants are influencing the leader's activities, decision, behavior, actions, and directions."

"When the leader is biased with some sycophants then organization rewards, awards, and gives perks, benefits, and opportunities to them. When the career of other people is jeopardized to groom the career of these sycophants or when other people are harassed and humiliated to satisfy their ego, it's nepotism."

"Well described Nikhil, it's a different perspective of nepotism in offices and this is really scary. So far I use to think that giving preference to your friend and family members is only nepotism. But in reality, when you destroy the career of others due to your preferences is a real problem of nepotism." Avantika said and it looks like for some time she forgot Sushant's issue, I never liked her sad face, she is the lifeline of our home.

"Yes, I believe having a preference is a separate issue. It's the leader's prerogative to whom they want to select and give the benefits. But it should not be done at other people's cost. If the owner's family and friends are capable to take the role, then they should be given but if you are giving the preference to non-deserving people, then you are promoting the nepotism in the organization."

"Correct Nikhil, it's an interesting discussion. I think it has been a long time we discussed any interesting thing." – Avantika.

"True Avantika, we both are busy nowadays. Your breaking news has allowed us to discuss something constructive."

Check out the following questions to see whether you are promoting nepotism at the workplace or not.

- Do you have preferred people and by default, they are entitled to get every rising opportunity?
- Have you built your core team based on merits and capabilities or based on your comfort and preferences?
- For how long you have not made any change in your core team?
- Do you accommodate new people in your core team?
- Does your existing team members of the core team become apprehensive as soon as you introduce any new person to the team?
- Can you promote any of your core team members without promoting the others? Or in other words, do you need to do babysitting for all your core team members.
- Do you give feedback to your core team members?
- Have you ever been forced to take any decision just to make your core team happy on which you were not aligned?
- Have you ever got a feeling that your core team is now a white elephant, and you have carried that weight?

"Nepotism is the lowest and least imaginative form of corruption"

-Daniel Alarcon

12

Haan Main Hoon Leader

SELF PROCLAIMED LEADERS

"When people give themselves a leadership title out of the circumstances without any merit, or endorsement by others."

Everyone in the leadership profile thinks they are a leader. It's common for people to associate "leadership" with a title. A Director is a "leader", the Creative Head is a "leader", even your manager is a "leader." But that's not what leadership actually is. Leadership isn't a badge you wear or a hat you put on in certain situations.

Why people are so desperate for a leadership profile? The simple answer is "to control" anything to everything whether it's people, their career, system, process, decision making, money, business, benefits, perks, or whatever they can control. That's the core reason to gain any position in the leadership profile. Another strong reason is the feeling of 'power' where 300 people are reporting to you. You have the power to decide the fate of these people whether to hire or fire them. You have the power to decide your growth and career plan. Being a leader gives you some extra perks like a bigger cabin in the office, executive class while traveling, people tend to be polite and respectful to you. The most common answers when you ask people **why are you a leader?**

- I am a born leader.
- My designation belongs to the leadership profile.
- I am the most experienced person in the company.
- I am the owner of a company.
- I am a subject matter expert, knows the nitty-gritty of this domain.
- I am from the first group of the company's employee when it was started, *apna khoon pasena lagya hai* (I have worked hard)
- I know how to handle people.
- *Saheb ka khas hoon, unka bahut bharosa hai mujh par* (I am favorite of boss and he trust me a lot).
- It's my father's company.
- Sudden demand arises to manage people, clients, operations, or projects in the organization so I have been given the responsibility to lead. (For example, "You're a great salesperson. Can you manage the team as well?", "You're a brilliant developer. Can you manage some projects, too?")
- I have been rewarded for my loyalty to management.
- Sheer luck. Being in the right place at the right time

And the list is endless to claim that they are the leader. Unfortunately, most of them are far from leadership. And the harsh reality is even many of us are in leadership profile just because of these reasons.

However, it's not the reason but the circumstances that push people to the leadership profile. If leadership is driven out of circumstances it's "Accidental Leadership". Nobody will admit that they are accidental leaders and the truth is, not everyone can or should become a leader. One can have a desire to be a leader but without any character, skill, and courage it is not feasible. Your circumstances can give you the title, force people to call you 'Sir/Madam' but whether people accept you as a leader or not it completely depends upon your skills. How will you know that are you an accidental leader or not? The things which are mentioned below, did they happen to you?

Do you need to remind people often about your title to get things done?

- Do you feel insecure about your position and title most of the time, rather than working towards the bigger goals?
- Do you often make more promises than keeping them?
- Do you believe in maintaining the status quo or breaking them?
- Do you feel insecure hiring or working with people who are more talented than you?

- Do you claim credit for all the work or pass it down to your people?
- Do you care about the process more than people?
- Do you prefer to immediately react to people in challenging situations and believe it's the best practice for giving instant feedback?
- Are you emotionally inconsistent?
- Do you point the finger instead of pulling the thumb?
- Do you focus more on the bad parts rather than highlighting the good part?
- Do you love to spend more time doing hands-on work?
- Do you see people's questions as interruptions?
- Do you fix mistakes rather than teaching?
- Do you feel people won't be able to perfectly finish the work without your two-cent advice?
- Do you get irritated when you are being held accountable for your people's work?
- Do you tend to avoid people who disagree with you?
- Do people tend to avoid you due to your unpredictable behavior?
- Do you always feel that you are right or even the smartest person in the room during any meeting or discussion?
- Do you think your customer also need your guidance and two-cent advice to run their businesses and do you often do that?
- Do you love keeping things ambiguous rather than clarifying so based on the outcome you can take credit or pass the blame on others?

If most of the answers are "Yes" then you are an "Accidental Leader". Maybe many of us are still in a dilemma that they are a leader or accidental one, okay let's evaluate the key question. Are you able to inspire people to do things they wouldn't do on their own?

Many people think even if they are accidental leaders what's the problem with it, they have a title, carry authority and people are reporting to them, what else they need. This procrastination comes from the survival attitude and true leaders don't work to survive they work to thrive. When a leader thrives, their people get inspired and engaged, and with such a workforce clients and businesses get benefited. It's a win-win situation. So it's up to us that even if circumstances have pushed us into the leadership domain, we can turn around the table by putting in some effort and can come out as a true leader.

Why people need leaders? Because they are unable to achieve what they want, they are directionless for their growth, or unable to identify their potential. They might not have the skills, the courage, the creativity, or the time. So they choose a leader who can help them to achieve.

An accidental leader not only damages their career prospect, but they can also ruin the career of their people. You may agree or disagree with these leaders but the harsh reality is that they hold the opportunities of their team members. They become the decision-maker for people as they decide on their work assignments, promotions, organization resources, onsite opportunities, perks & benefits, etc. As they are accidental leaders, their decisions are not driven by the people's performance, their abilities, and the organization's future need. Rather it is driven by their convenience and survival approach. This eventually damages their future as well because they are not putting the right people in right place and at right time, resulting in limited or less organizational growth which ultimately limits their prospect to grow as well. They are often indecisive, unable to connect with people, lack the necessary social skills, and are not sufficiently resilient.

So it's time to rethink for accidental leaders whether they want to live in the illusion of being a leader as they don't have anything to lose because of the title and circumstances, but they forget circumstances can change at any time. Neither leaders are born nor leadership is gifted by the titles, it has to be built. One can, however, overcome this problem by better preparing themselves for leadership.

Many of us think that leadership is an individual problem and doesn't impact the organization. However, the reality is different, and when you start looking into the statistics available then you may understand the importance of leadership development in the company. If you are observing the following challenges within the organization then you need to seriously think about leadership development.

- The leadership team is unable to either set the goals or unable to achieve the target for more than three years continuously
- More hierarchies, unnecessary process
- No accountability among the leadership team
- No conviction about the business goals
- Grapevine communication is more prominent than structured communication

Poor leadership not only costs millions of dollars for the companies each year but also creates an adverse impact on employee retention, engagement and productivity, and customer satisfaction.

According to Research from the Blanchard Company

- Less-than-optimal leadership practices cost the typical organization an amount equal to as much as 7% of their total annual sales
- At least 9% and possibly as much as 32% of an organization's staff turnover can be avoided through better leadership skills
- Better leadership can generate a 3-4% improvement in customer satisfaction scores and a corresponding 1.5% increase in revenue growth
- Most organizations are operating with a 5-10% productivity drag that better leadership practices could eliminate

According to Gallup

- It's a sad truth about the workplace: just 30% of employees are actively committed to doing a good job.
- Gallup's 2013 State of the American Workplace report indicates that 50% of employees merely put their time in, while the remaining 20% act out their discontent in counterproductive ways, negatively influencing their coworkers, missing days on the job, and driving customers away through poor service.
- Gallup estimates that the 20% group alone costs the U.S. economy around half a trillion dollars each year.

The single greatest cause for all of the above facts? ***Poor leadership.***

It's simple, the better the leader, the more engaged the employee, the more engaged employee will love their job and when people love what they do, they become more productive resulting in great customer satisfaction. That's what everyone's goals are.

In the traditional approach, leadership profiles are being considered based on the number of people are reporting to them. We all are learning pyramid structure or hierarchy from the ages where leaders are sitting on top and the higher they are, the more authority they have. Leaders in a pyramid structure rule the organization like a king and people having a difference of opinion with leadership are considered enemies.

The foundation of the traditional model is to blame and outsources the responsibility of failed decisions and action to team members. In this

model leaders proudly delegates their responsibilities to others and it remains with them unless it reaches any outcome. If the outcome is positive leaders are ready to take credit and if in case of negative results others will continue to carry the responsibilities. Leaders are only to command others and exercise their authority in the traditional approach.

The traditional model of leadership badly impacts the organizational culture where people, processes, and systems are working to keep the leader's leadership intact rather than growing business, people, and customers. Organizational culture lies below the surface of observable behavior and includes how leaders make decisions, how they deal with authority, and how they communicate.

Time has changed, nowadays the secret of any successful business is team efforts, collaboration, and cohesive working conditions. The "traditional" approach rarely thrives on any sizeable scale. Today, it is the demand of visionary leaders who have big ideas and, most importantly, can inspire people around them to turn those ideas into reality.

Leaders are expected to come up with ideas and creative solutions and promote the team to utilize these ideas to grow their career and subsequently the organization. If you will see around most of the businesses under the traditional leadership, it keeps standing still and competitors are constantly growing. Over time, a static and conservative approach of leadership leads to a challenge where customers and employees are migrating to their competitors.

Change has become the norm today. It is very apparent that the world we work and live in is constantly changing and the only solution to keep up with the changing demands is to have the right leaders in place who can take responsibility for inspiring and engaging the team to promote changes. Besides today's millennial workforce are the incredibly ethically-conscious generation and regard ethics and values higher than a generous salary. Millennials want to work for a leader that makes a positive impact and they work harder if they know their work is making a difference in the world.

Therefore, you need a leader who can instead of deflecting, choose to take responsibility for fixing the problem and work on it to the ground. The blame model is not at all ethical and doesn't create any value. People love to work with leaders who take responsibility, as it creates an environment of trust. If a leader is taking responsibility for work, issues, and problems it shows that he is trusting the team, even if it is not directly their fault.

Today's workforce is smarter and observant. They closely monitor their leaders' behavior and can easily identify if leaders play the blame model. Responsibility is not what defines in KRA of leaders, it's a mindset that says "I am the person who must make this happen". Today's millennial workforce won't accept the 'authority' of leaders unless they take the 'responsibility', practically if you see leadership has only 'responsibility', not 'authority'.

By designing the pyramid structure, people down the line carry the burden of leadership and leaders who are commanding the team. This structure puts pressure on the people to make leaders' decisions successful and in case of any issues and challenges, these people are impacted the most.

This approach keeps less burden on leaders for their responsibilities and people are required to take all the load to fulfill it.

The question is what rectification is required to improvise this structure where we can make the leaders more responsible for their decisions and actions. We see the pyramid structure doesn't fit in today's demanding and competitive world, in terms of bringing growth for leaders themselves, their people, and the organization.

The organizations are required to restructure in it a wheel form where leaders are kept in the center and people are in the periphery of the wheel. The center of the wheel carries the weight and is responsible for keeping it rolling. Similarly, when leaders are kept in the center of the wheel they become responsible for their decisions, as the outcome of their decisions will directly hit the momentum of the wheel. This structure won't allow the blame to pass on to other people, responsibility is on the leaders' shoulders.

So having the wheel-like organization structure can help to overcome accidental leadership as it is designed in such a way that it will fail if accidental leaders are roped in.

Many people start reading various leadership books, some do online courses and some attend workshops as soon as they get into the leadership domain. All approaches are good to immediately gain the know-how of the leadership domain. Different books can give you a different perspective, sometime you may be able to find the answers to your leadership challenges and sometimes not. Leadership is not binary which can be bind with a set of rules to apply and practice. There are certain dos and don'ts but one has to apply that based on their environment. A rule which has worked in one environment may fail in another. So books and courses can give you the knowledge but won't help you to effectively manage your day-to-day challenges.

You need all combinations of learning and grooming to become a successful player in any of the games. Players get groomed over a period before they become seasoned. Their evolution is depending on their practices, reading, and learning techniques, attending expert workshops. However, the biggest secret lies in the success of a player, it's a coach. Yes, you read it correctly "Coach". It would be hard to imagine any sports team or professional athlete getting by without a coach.

You may be wondering why a leader needs a coach. Most leadership books and training programs focus on how leaders can achieve more—do more, better, faster, with spectacular results. But they rarely focus on how to deal with the challenges or what are the leadership traps. Fortunately, we have covered in this book but still, no book or program can directly address your challenges. All these things are one-way communication, no one is listening to you or your challenges. Then how can you expect to resolve it by reading and attending it. Hence, you need a coach like any sportsperson. There are so many parallels you can draw between business and sport such as the drive for success, high performance, and the need to go beyond perceived limits.

A coach encourages you to see things with another set of eyes' and helps you in gaining a renewed perspective on any given issue. A coach works for you and with you to help you reach the best vision for yourself. Coach encourages a "forced focus" on what is the most important to you versus the constant distraction of the urgent. Everyone has a blind spot but if you don't know what it is, you will continue to undermine your success.

And the most important thing is that a coach never works against you, the success of a coach is determined by the success of people to whom they are coaching. Your boss, colleague, or friend can be your mentor or buddy but they cannot be a coach because they will have some or other conflict of interest as their paths are also crossing your path. Identify the independent coach who can help you to transform from an accidental leader to a true leader. A coach can help you

- **To become your soundboard:** The coach will listen to you, your problems, accomplishment, challenges and can give you the other perspective which helps you in taking better decisions.
- **To give feedback:** As a leader, you might not receive feedback on your decisions, actions, or approach. A coach can not only give you feedback but also help to integrate the feedback for specific actions.
- **To keep you focused:** Mostly leadership is an independent profile. Leaders work in autopilot mode and easily get distracted as they have multiple things to do. And there is always a thin line between getting things done or doing things on their own. A coach knows what the priority for you is as per your goals or vision and helps you to remain focused accordingly.

However, not anyone can become your coach to help you in improving your leadership skills. Don't assume your reporting manager or a friend or someone senior can be your coach. You need to look for a coach who is an expert in the leadership domain and willing to coach you. For many people, mentors and coaches are the same things. However, mentors are experienced and trusted advisors and coaches will work with you as a partner in a thought-provoking and creative process that inspires you to maximize your personal and professional potential.

Leadership is a difficult role and everyone needs leadership skills to grow in their career, it's not a skill that is required by only business owners or C- level executives. Everyone is an owner of their work, and CEO of their brand, hence they need to lead and effectively manage their work. Leadership is an essential skill irrespective of your profile or position in the organizational structure. Great leadership skills will not only help you professionally but will also help in your personal life. As a parent, spouse, brother, sister, a friend you are always trying to lead in different situations to help your family, friends, and society.

No one is born as a leader, instead, it happens gradually, and thus everyone commits mistakes in their leadership journey.

ACKNOWLEDGMENT

- **Yugank Kulshrestha,** *@yugankkulshresth,* **Naitra Kulshrestha,** *@ naitra_kulshrestha,* and **Nidhi Jain,** *@nidhi9775.* For reviewing and editing the book.
- **Nishant Mevada,** *@nishart_66.* For designing caricature and diagrams.
- **Shradha Ahuja Ramani,** *@shradhaahujaramani.* For guiding us in publishing the book.
- **Mandar Mukadam,** *@mandarmukadam* and **Rituraj,** *@rtr026.* For cover design.
- **Tanmay Jain,** *@_tman._* For Layout and Design
- **Maya Khudabadi,** *@mayakhudabadi* & **Business Mantra,**

  @businessmantra.m. For the marketing of the book.
- And to the various source of the **Internet.**

above are the instagram handles

FROM AUTHORS

Vishal Kulshrestha

I come from a typical middle-class family and was born and brought up in small-town Kota, Rajsthan, known for Engineering & Medical coaching. My life is not different from any other middle-class person, first who studies to get a good job, once gets a job, then work hard to step-up in a career, upgrades lifestyle with the support of EMI based economy.

I may be the last generation who were blessed to listen stories from their grandparents, and as I grew up and I found stories are the best source for learning. It easily connects me with the subject, before understanding 'How' it tells 'What happened' and then understanding 'how' becomes easy. Stories activate the senses and emotions, gives you an experience, and take you into an artificial reality, either you want to learn or want to make someone else learn, it's the best approach to follow.

Writing a book always was on my bucket list, until I met Siddharth it was just a wish. We found common synergy and thoughts about leadership and decided to compile all real-life stories which either we experienced or people we met experienced, to share with the community.

Professionally I am in IT services, serving the industry for the last 22 years playing various roles. By nature, I am a conversationalist and observant. I am an active blogger and an advocate of servant leadership.

You can follow me *@kulshresthavk* on Instagram or Twitter or follow #StoryTellerVK on social media for interesting updates on leadership and management.

Siddharth Gaur

I am a product of the '80s from a small city of Rajasthan, Sikar. Initially, I was a civil service aspirant and spent the golden youth years pursuing that dream. Those days made me who I am today. I developed two main traits of my personality in those days. Reading and constant learning. My reading habit of those days eventually turned into a passion for writing.

When destiny gave me the chance to have corporate exposure I took every bit of it to learn. Learned by observing. I keenly observed the leaders around me, the established once and the wanna-bes. My profile as an HR professional allowed me to associate with people closely and to hear, understand and guide.

Writing a book is harder than I thought and more rewarding than I could have ever imagined. None of this would have been possible without my best friend Ajay Nirwan. He motivated and even forced me to write a book long back from our College days.

I am eternally thankful to my close buddies Sq leader Dushyant Rathore,Pankaj Sharma, Jitesh Jalan, and Nikhil Mathur for reading early drafts, giving me advice, and sharing experiences from their respective workplaces.

I am forever indebted to my co-author Vishal who initiated the idea to write this book. While being on different continents for most of the time during writing this book it was him who never let us both slow down and kept the coordination intact.

To my family for their encouragement.

To all the individuals I have had the opportunity to lead, be led by, or watch their leadership from afar. I want to say thank you for being the inspiration and foundation for the leader sinks ship.